THE

EXORDIUM

BOOKS ONE TO FOUR
(VOLUME I)

THE EMERGENCE
OF THE GODS

MEHDI
ZAND

The possibility that is certain

Yaad Publications

Second Edition, 1st printing

First published in Great Britain in 2004 by Yaad Publications,
PO Box 2111, WD17 4XQ, United Kingdom.

www.worldofyaad.org
www.mehdizand.org

British Library Cataloguing in Publication Data:
A catalogue record for this book is available from the British Library

ISBN 0 9547254 1 7

DEDICATION

I, Mehdi Zand, dedicate this book to you, the reader, so you can follow the wisdom of the gods and you can enter the new time of celestial understanding. Hopefully, these words of mystery will ignite your inner consciousness and enlighten your heart towards the fire, the fire of the divine intelligence. May the power of the first name bless those who read the words of truth and all those who walk on the path of unity and light.

So let it be written.

Let it be done.

Exordium I

Contents

BOOK FOUR - THE UNDERWORLD: THE INTELLIGENCES OF FIRE

An Introduction To The Exordium

Do you know why you chose to read this book? Was it because you have heard of its writer, Mehdi Zand? Was it because the Exordium was recommended to you, or because you have heard the controversy surrounding it? Did you pick up this book because its cover caught your eye and you wondered what this unknown fire was? Or instead, did the Exordium call out to you?

So, do you know what you are holding in your hand? You are holding the story that has never been told before. You are holding the mysteries that are so deep that no philosopher, no scholar, no mystic and no prophet has ever dared to imagine. You are holding the emergence and the history of the gods.

From the moment that Man first began to think, he has wondered who he is and where he has come from. Since then, he has invented gods and demons to explain the world and his existence. Some of these powers he called good, and others evil; some became known as the friends of man, others his enemy. People have come, claiming to be the prophets or messengers of these hidden beings. Mankind has created religions to safeguard the souls of the masses and given clergy the power to hold the keys to the gates of 'heaven'. Throughout history, Man has killed and destroyed one another in the name of these gods. And meanwhile, these gods have remained silent, as if they never existed...

What Man has imagined may not be real, but there are gods that *do* exist, and the Exordium is their story.

Read this book. Imagine the chapters. Hear the voices of the gods. See through their eyes and experience their emotions. Live the Exordium.

Is this book heresy? Most definitely. Is it real? That is for you to decide.

Welcome to the Exordium. The gods are waiting.

Notes to the Second Edition

This edition of the Exordium is a simplified version of the original. It has been written to bring the beauty of the Exordium to a wider audience.

OPENING

WELCOME

Welcome.

Welcome to the realistic past of the aeon.

Welcome to the solidness of unwritten history.

Welcome to the dynamic particles of the hidden time.

Welcome to the unimagined domain of the hidden intelligences who became the original formation of existence and the seed for the present reality as we know today.

INVITATION

This is an invitation, an invitation into the heart of fire, so I, Mehdi Zand, can take you beyond the frontier of the hidden mind, into the region where the particles of age were the centre of inconsistency, into the sphere of the forgotten time where the mystical characteristics of the chaos were strategising to conquer the future law of existence.

This is an invitation, an invitation into the domain of universal mystery that no other man has dared to contemplate.

This is an invitation, an invitation into the ultimate essence of reality, into the heart of the realistic dream, into the origin of the divine imagination, the imagination as real as the face of the Sun and as deep as the depths of the rising ocean.

Exordium I

Now, I invite you once again. I invite every soul of fire, every intelligence of integrity and every inhabitant of this limitless universe of touch into the depths of my rising mind, into the centre of my imagination, into the mysterious emergence of the so-called gods of the ancient aeon, into the formation of mystery, into the core of reality, into the fire of beginning, into the Exordium.

Book One

The Totality Of
The First Universe

THE FIRST DECLARATION OF THE ESSER YAAD[1], THE DIVINE FIRE OF GOD

A long time ago, before the universe began to exist as we know today, when the first hidden confrontation was over, when the victory of the constructive forces of divinity was completed, I looked upon My victorious allies and My defeated opponents and said,

"One day, I will present the absolute seal[2] of power in the midst of the images of God to glorify and spread My real name and to portray the greatest conflict that has ever taken place in the history of universal evolution."

I promised that one day, as the host of the living fire of existence, I would glorify and honour the ancient gods of the past and, with the excellence of My celestial magic, awaken every other metaphysical force of divinity from the state of oblivion.

Now, let us enter into the fire, into the beginning. Let us enter into the Exordium.

So be it.

---

[1] Esser Yaad: the first fire of divinity; the power that we recognise as the Lord God
[2] Seal: a stamp of authority; an image or writing used for magic

INTRODUCTION TO CHAPTER 1
THE MAIN CONCENTRATED INTELLIGENCE

The Superconsciousness, or the main concentrated intelligence, is what I call the Godhead. As it is written, He is the first-ever consciousness that came out of the void of nothingness. He is the solidness of life and the path to immortality. His image is the hidden flames of fire. No one can define the nature of His existence as He stands above every image of thought and any source of imagination.

The Superconsciousness, or the Godhead, is the unseen architect of this touchable reality. He is the beginning of the creative mind and the ultimate path to awakening consciousness.

We should comprehend that there are many levels of creation and a multitude of dimensions that are interconnected by the Superconsciousness, who coordinates the progress of every living organism. He is the absolute solidity and the creator of what we call the cause.

Now as we will see, the Superconsciousness, or the Godhead, was the self-manifested image of mystery, intelligent and highly sophisticated, able to think and to imagine the emptiness. Everything begins like this.

This Force that we recognise as the Godhead somehow came out of nothingness, into the certain region – some form of void that He may have imagined. Then He began to imagine the emptiness. Why? So He could fill this space with His imagination. Within His imagination lies the universe as we know today.

Exordium I

Enjoy the manifestation of the main concentrated intelligence. He came forth out of nothingness. He broke every barrier of thought. He is invincible, unimaginable. He is the Godhead of the Exordium.

CHAPTER ONE

THE MAIN CONCENTRATED INTELLIGENCE

Part 1: This is before the realisation of time, before the emergence of the light, before the beginning began to exist as we know today.

There was no effective formation. There was no solidness of reality. There was no structure of identity. All there was, was nothingness.

For millions of hidden years, the condition of the unseen universe was like this. Eventually, from the centre of this nothingness, from the heart of this void of the unknown, came forth the self-generated and self-manifested intelligence who beheld the entire foundation of universal consciousness.

Part 2: This intelligence was in the image of the concentrated circle of mystery. Right in the middle of this circle was a second sphere, the sphere of the golden flames of fire.

Part 3: This concentrated form of intelligence stayed motionless and thoughtful for many cycles of aeon[1]. His intention was to measure the heaviness of His being and balance the force of electricity that was stored within Him.

This concentrated image of intelligence, with the power of His dynamic will, eventually emerged out of the centre of

---

[1] Aeon: time

nothingness. His first station was some form of void. There He began to imagine the emptiness.

He imagined the emptiness so, by the duration of age, He could fill this globe of emptiness with the countless number of future particles of life.

This concentrated form of intelligence began to move cautiously. His intention was to analyse the limit of His power and reach the other end of the so-called existence.

Many cycles of time passed inconsistently. The Superconsciousness, or the main concentrated intelligence, began to mobilise and release His thought-forms into the space that He had imagined. He did this to construct the first strategy of creation.

Introduction to Chapter 2
Gravity

Gravity, as it will be noticed, was formed for the purpose of stability and evenness. The formation of gravity exists in its original form. Although it is the necessary centre of magnetism pulling the elements to the Earth, it is still performing its original duty: keeping every entity away from one another and from the hidden form of the main concentrated intelligence, the Godhead.

We can look at gravity as the problems of life pulling us down into day-to-day activities and the complexities of the environment. As conscious souls, we should dedicate certain periods of our time to recognise the reason for our existence and the essence of our becoming. We should be aware not to become a victim of this hidden vortex, the gravity.

Now, can you visualise the hidden form of the Godhead imagining the space of the emptiness, floating and thinking in this domain of the unknown? His thought-forms are beginning to spread. He selects certain groups of His thought-forms and from them He removes the element of thoughtfulness. Then He projects some of His heaviness into their empty shells so they can move beneath His structure and create the force-field of stability to enable Him to float evenly. Gravity was formed.

Enjoy the chapter.

Chapter Two

Gravity

Part 1: Time did not exist as we know it today. The particles of aeon may have moved, but their motion was unconscious and their sequences were inconsistent.

As these unconscious particles of time were passing inconsistently, the Superconsciousness, through the analysation of His surroundings, realised the necessity for a certain force-field of power.

Part 2: His intention was to construct this force-field so He could float evenly and hover without losing His original momentum of stability.

Then the Superconsciousness began to think within this domain that He imagined. His thinking created the ocean of thought-forms: some imaginative, some creative, some progressive and some resistant to any power other than His own.

The Superconsciousness, or the main concentrated intelligence, began to select certain legions of these resisting thought-forms and from them He removed the elements of thoughtfulness. Soon these legions were without the element of thought, but maintained the empty images of floating thought-forms.

Part 3: The Superconsciousness strategically projected a portion of His heaviness into the centre of these empty images of floating thought-forms.

After this calculated operation, He began to force all these heavy void-like thought-forms outside His very self, into the domain of emptiness.

These void-like thought-forms began to spread, and some, as He strategised, floated beneath His hidden being and created the force-field of symmetrical evenness.

Gravity was formed.

Introduction to Chapter 3
Hydrogen

Hydrogen is one of the most plentiful elements in the universe. The mechanism of hydrogen bonding was the instrument that the Superconsciousness (the Godhead) and the Esser Yaad (the Lord God) used to create the physical and metaphysical entities. Through the application of this mechanism, by increasing or decreasing the number and structure of certain genetic ingredients such as chromosomes, the shape and image of the body can be made to differ. As the result of this equation, countless number of different species are scattered across the entirety of the universe; those we can see and those we cannot.

Read and enjoy the third chapter of the Exordium.

———————————

Chapter Three

Hydrogen

Part 1: After the formation of gravity, the sensation within the surrounding domain began to change. The void-like thought-forms began to spread, and their movement created a certain force-field with the power to sustain the forthcoming elements evenly in the invisible space of emptiness.

Part 2: As the particles of time were not passing consistently in the manner that is now generally recognised, the gravity was also not responding methodically in accordance to the scientific understanding and analysation of today.

These void-like thought-forms were acting in reverse. Rather than being the core of magnetism to pull down the elements towards the magnetic centre, they were a force-field to push every intelligence away from one another. As a result, every intelligence could stay seperate and float evenly and symmetrically.

Part 3: With the patterns of the void-like thought-forms assembled in place and the space of emptiness imagined accordingly, the Superconsciousness began to remove certain gaseous ingredients from the heart of His golden flames of fire.

Then the Superconsciousness, or the main concentrated intelligence, began to collect all the gaseous ingredients together to form one massive sphere with the flammable capability.

Part 4: After the formation of this flammable sphere, the Superconsciousness forcefully ejected this globe of gaseous ingredients into the space of emptiness. This globe had three original missions to accomplish. First, to multiply and become the substance to arrange the genetic ingredients for the future structure of any form of intelligence. Second, to create the original base for the electrification of matter. Third, to produce visible and invisible forms of universal radiation.

The initial bonding of hydrogen was formed.

INTRODUCTION TO CHAPTER 4
OXYGEN

Oxygen is one of the most important substances in the science of biochemical engineering. Its importance is highly recognised on Earth as the continuation of human life and almost every other organism depends upon the presence of this hidden circuit.

Read this chapter and see how mysteriously the element of oxygen found its own intended duty. Follow the Exordium.

———————————

Chapter Four

Oxygen

Part 1: The gravity was formed. The element of hydrogen began its own mysterious mission. The Superconsciousness, or the main concentrated intelligence, began to float upon this limitless void in the perfect mode of symmetrical evenness.

Part 2: After many cycles of hidden time passed inconsistently, the Superconsciousness began to remove yet another chemical ingredient from the centre of His golden flames of fire. The intention of the Superconsciousness was to collect certain elemental substances that could become the cause of ignition.

Part 3: When this systematic act was complete, the Superconsciousness assembled all these chemical substances together to construct another magnified globe of atomic ingredients. This magnified globe had the capability to penetrate into the midst of the emptiness and gradually encompass the hidden layers of many floating atmospheres.

Part 4: After the construction of this sphere, the Superconsciousness methodically ejected this globe into the imagined space of emptiness. This globe had three universal missions to accomplish: first, to multiply and become one of the organic substances that would combine with most existing elements; second, to spread evenly and transform into the specific flammable factor; and third, to be the invisible gaseous component, essential for the respiration of any existing organism. The hidden circuit of oxygen was formed.

Introduction to Chapter 5
The Lord Of Constructive Fire

This is the first emergence of the Lord of constructive fire, the Esser Yaad, who became the ultimate manifestation of the Superconsciousness.

In this chapter, He is in the form of the flaming fire of genesis. Holding within the centre of His being the power of the entire thoughtfulness, He begins to strategise the patterns for the future construction of the physical universe.

This Lord of constructive fire is above the conception of time. The duration of age has no effect upon His flames of integrity. He was present within the reality of every event, and He still exists within the totality of every single intelligent organism.

As the power of infinite consciousness, He holds the actual solidness of life. In the Exordium, He is the first god of the ancient aeon who, as part of the Godhead, emerged out of the void of nothingness. In the hidden history of the universe, He is the soul of the unknown. He is the creative mind who fills the imagination of the Godhead and constructs the strategy of resurrection. He is the effect of the thought and the cause behind the manifestation of the divine will.

For us to discover His excellence and glory, we should proceed towards our spiritual and metaphysical progression. Only then can we reach this ultimate flame of fire and comprehend His quest for perfection: the divinity.

In this chapter, the Esser Yaad begins to create His original form. He collects every necessary ingredient of thoughtfulness and then projects His gigantic image into the space of emptiness. Do you know what this means? It means the force that we call God constructed His voyage to reach the very end of endlessness. Can you visualise the greatness of this mystery? Can you imagine this unbelievable structure of fire proceeding into the void of imagination? He goes further and further until He reaches the centre of emptiness. There He stands evenly and symmetrically, ready to construct His next creative strategy.

Follow the Exordium; the Exordium is the new concept of philosophy.

CHAPTER FIVE

THE LORD OF CONSTRUCTIVE FIRE

Part 1: The imagined domain of emptiness was getting ready to be filled by the creative mind of the Lord of the constructive fire. How did it all begin?

Part 2: Right at the centre of the main concentrated intelligence, or the Godhead, certain raging flames of fire became volcanically activated. They began to collect every ingredient of constructive thoughtfulness, every particle of atomic construction and every solid component of inner consciousness. They empowered their cosmic awareness and assembled every ray of intellect, every field of virtual imagination and every creative element of the mind to construct a massive structure of the awakened fire of life.

Part 3: This structure of fire regenerated the power of His mathematical intelligence. He multiplied His inner strength and created the force-field of radiation within the centre of His being.

Part 4: When these strategical ingatherings of the divine attributes were completed, this gigantic globe of the awakened fire projected Himself out of the main concentrated intelligence, or the Godhead, into the void of emptiness.

Part 5: Then one of the most mysterious voyages of pre-galactical history began. This structure of the awakened fire of life proceeded into the midst of the imagined emptiness, into the vast and limitless void of the unknown, into the land where the boundaries had no solidness of recognition. This massive structure of fire penetrated into the zone of the twilight. He went further and further, deeper and deeper, until He reached the very centre of this spreading emptiness.

Part 6: When He reached the centre of this spreading emptiness, He floated evenly and symmetrically above the layers of the hidden atmosphere.

When He found the correct and suitable ground to formulate His hidden intention, He began to strategise His constructive thought-forms correctly and dynamically.

The very point, the domain of stability and the ground for the future creation of His own divine image (the universal soul of fire), was discovered.

CHAPTER SIX

LET US ENTER

Part 1: Now let us enter into the zone where the solidness of the first soul of intelligence was constructed, into the time when the hidden structure of the divine manifestation emerged from the concentrated flames of the urging fire.

Let us enter into the era when the first god of the ancient aeon stood above the plane of emptiness and became the only mind behind the constructive evolution of the universe.

Now let us enter into the unwritten history when every flame of rising intellect joined together and changed their volcanic images into one exalted soul, the soul of divinity.

Part 2: Now let us enter into the sphere of hidden oxygen, into the abode of the flammable element of hydrogen where this unified fire of the rising intellect became the first god of all. He used the exact proportion of chemical substances to create His organs, His torso, His limbs, His neck, His head, His inner brain and the mystical form of His facial appearance.

Let us enter into the height of mystery and follow the self-transformation of this ultimate fire of life into the hidden form of power that we recognise as the Lord God.

Part 3: Now let us enter into the uncalculated sphere of time when this Lord of constructive fire stood forcefully, majestically, with the mysterious image of outstretched divinity[1] in the midst of the domain of the unknown, the emptiness.

---

[1] Outstretched divinity: the image of a person standing with their feet apart and arms stretched out to the sides

27

Introduction to Chapter 7
The Language Of Fire

The language of fire is the most mysterious, powerful and ancient language of all. Its alphabetical characters are alive. They are the necessary ingredients for the procedure of magic. This language is connected to the very depths of our central brain and is the most important mechanism to enter the other existing dimensions.

Mastery of this language is the key to understand the phenomena of the unseen and the passage to comprehend the sacred keys of universal consciousness. It should be noticed that learning this language can take you one step closer to the reality of higher evolution.

Now when you read this chapter, you should concentrate attentively. Try to imagine the situation. Feel the clashing orbits of fire. Try to hear the volcanic sound of these rising flames of integrity. You are in the centre of the formation, the formation of the most mysterious language of all. Use the gift of your imagination correctly. Only then will you begin to appreciate the uniqueness of this chapter.

Enjoy the Exordium.

Chapter Seven

Chapter Seven

The Language Of Fire

Part 1: The journey continued when the Lord of constructive fire reached the centre of the emptiness and stayed evenly above the layers of this invisible and hidden atmosphere.

Part 2: Then this gigantic fire of existence began to analyse the entire surroundings. As the particles of time were passing inconsistently and inaccurately, He realised the important factor: to formulate certain verbal mechanisms so that He could converse with His higher self.

Part 3: So this constructive Lord of fire used His inner hearing to differentiate the variety of the clashing flames of fire that were constantly activating within His very self.

Part 4: He concentrated in the perfect mode of precision and named each sound of these clashing flames accordingly.

Part 5: Then He divided their sounds into three recognisable categories.

Those flames of fire which were volcanically rising, He named them 'magnetic vermilion'. Those flames which were circulating in the mysterious way, He named them 'dynamic cerulean'. And those which were at the base, regenerating the seed of continuity, He named them the 'fundamental citrine'.

Part 6: The first and the most mysterious language of fire was formed, the language of Ser-ra.

INTRODUCTION TO CHAPTER 8
I AM WHAT I AM

After the formation of the language of Ser-ra, the first-ever inner conversation took place between the Esser Yaad (the Lord of constructive fire) and His higher self. It is important to understand that this original dialogue is the first sign of self-realisation.

The Esser Yaad asks, "Who am I?"

The answer is: "I am the mind."

Why the mind? Because the mind is the most essential instrument of creation.

Then the next question: "The mind of what?"

His higher self answers, "The mind of the universe," as the universe is within Him; "The mind of fire," as He is the source of any rising flame of thought.

The Esser Yaad continues, "What am I?"

"I am the soul." The nature is unknown. "I am what I am."

That is the most mysterious answer we can find. 'I' is the certainty of the self, and the 'am' is the centre of the existence. Now read the entire conversation and see how the Esser Yaad recognises that He is the likeness of the first-ever image of divinity. He is the totality, the totality of oneness.

Chapter Eight

I Am What I Am

Part 1: After the completion of the most mysterious and sacred language of all, this Lord of constructive fire began to analyse the entire surrounding of emptiness. As there was no sound except the voice of His own clashing flames of fire, He formulated the first-ever inner conversation with His higher self in this manner of presentation:

1. "Who am I?

    "I am the mind.

2. "The mind of what?

    "The mind of the universe. The mind of fire.

3. "What am I?

    "I am the essence. I am the soul. The soul is what I am. I am what I am."

Part 2: The Lord of fire continued this mysterious conversation with His higher self in this calculated fashion:

1. "Where is this place of emptiness?

    "Within the realistic plane of imagination.

2. "What is the realistic plane of imagination?

    "The domain for the actual emergence of the divine manifestation.

3. "What is the divine manifestation?

    "The constructive awakening of the self.

4. "What is the constructive awakening of the self?

"The celestial attribute.

5. "What is the celestial attribute?

"The first image.

6. "What does the first image represent?

"The totality.

7. "The totality of what?

"The totality of oneness."

INTRODUCTION TO CHAPTER 9
THE MYSTICAL FORM OF THE SUPERCONSCIOUSNESS

Here this Lord of constructive fire concentrates to see the other end of the emptiness. There He sees the image of the main concentrated intelligence, the Superconsciousness (the Godhead). Then a series of questions and answers takes place within His rising flames of thought. If we follow the pattern of this chapter, we will recognise that the Esser Yaad has full understanding of His own characteristics and the absolute recognisation of the Superconsciousness.

CHAPTER NINE

THE MYSTICAL FORM OF THE SUPERCONSCIOUSNESS

Part 1: In this era of inconsistent time, this Lord of constructive fire used the power of sight to see and analyse the very end of this globe of emptiness. He concentrated for many cycles of aeon until His inner sight reached the ultimate edge of this hidden universe. There He saw the image of the main concentrated intelligence, the mystical form of the Superconsciousness.

Part 2: After seeing this majestic form, He raised His voice of power within His mind and formulated yet another mysterious conversation with His higher self in this manner of discourse:

1. "What is this concentrated cycle of mystery? I can feel the sensation of His fire.

"This is the main concentrated intelligence, or the image of the Superconsciousness, from whom I have separated Myself many aeons ago.

2. "What is the original function of the main concentrated intelligence?

"The functions of the main concentrated intelligence are many.

3. "Can You explain to Yourself the first constructive function of the Superconsciousness?

"The first constructive function is that He is the law. He is the law so the gravity can maintain any form of intelligence evenly and symmetrically on the surface of this domain of emptiness.

4. "Could You explicate to Yourself the second important function of the Superconsciousness?

"The second important function is that He is the principle behind the formation of hydrogen. The Superconsciousness is the cause for the electrification of matter and the intention behind the emergence of any metaphysical and physical intelligence.

5. "Would You elucidate to Yourself the third essential function behind the essence of the Superconsciousness?

"The third original function is that He is the motive for the structure of oxygen. He is the reason that this structure became the necessary particle for every explosion. His inner urge activates this component to be the element for the respiration of any living organism.

6. "Will You express to Yourself the fourth essential function regarding the totality of the Superconsciousness?

"The fourth essential function is that He is the intelligence behind the touchable imagination of reality. He is the motivation inviting My mind to construct the strategy of creation. The main concentrated intelligence is the all-present consciousness as He can be felt within every hidden particle of this spreading region of emptiness."

INTRODUCTION TO CHAPTER 10
HE IS ME IN THE HIDDEN FLESH OF FIRE

In this chapter, the strangest event takes place. This mighty fire, who is the totality of oneness, concentrates; and within the centre of the mind of the Superconsciousness, He sees the most mysterious, enigmatic and magnificent form of out-stretched divinity. After a certain amount of analysation, He realises that this mighty image of mystery is the image that the Superconsciousness (the Godhead) wants Him to be.

So what is this image? What significance does this image have? This image was in the shape of the celestial master standing above the altar of magic. We can imagine Homo sapiens to have the closest resemblance to this image today. That is why mankind is described as being 'in the similitude and the likeness of God' or the 'images of God'.

Now can you imagine what is going on within the mind of this constructive Lord of fire? Yes, this fire thinks dynamically and reaches the most important conclusion of all: this invincible, unimaginable structure of divinity is Himself in the hidden flesh of fire. Soon after this event, the series of the self-transformation of this mighty fire will begin.

Follow the Exordium.

CHAPTER TEN

HE IS ME IN THE HIDDEN
FLESH OF FIRE

Part 1: After the passing of many cycles of inconsistent time, this Lord of fire concentrated and looked into the depths of the heart of the Superconsciousness. There He saw an image: the structure of the future embodiment of divinity. It was enigmatic and mysterious, powerful and magnificent, mighty and majestic.

Part 2: He paused for a short cycle of aeon, trying to analyse the depths of this cosmic image of glory. Then this Lord of constructive fire raised His volcanic voice of integrity and said,

"What is this mysterious image of the unknown? What is this enigmatic face of magic that holds the principle of celestial eliteness? It is like the figure of reality standing above the solid ground of realisation. He looks like the embodiment of power, establishing the mastership of cosmic manifestation."

Part 3: This fire of existence continued His mysterious self-conversation in this manner of discourse:

"He must be the genesis of the force, or He may be the architect of this hidden domain of touch. He looks like the Word that I dreamed, and He is like the solidness of the Thought that I imagined. He must be the seed of the universal consciousness, or He may be the key to this mystic flame of philosophical thoughtfulness.

This Lord of constructive fire continued.

"This image seems to be invincible. I think it is one of a kind. Hmm."

(The sound of 'Hmm' resonated in the entire region of emptiness.)

"Let Me think. This is beyond the cosmic comprehension. This *must* be the image of mystery that holds the magic of creation. Let Me concentrate. *This* is what I should look like. This is the image that the Superconsciousness wants His ultimate manifestation to be. He is projecting it into My mind. I am removing it from the depths of His brain. This is the exact duplication, as it must be. Yes, this *is* My celestial likeness. He *is* Me in the hidden flesh of fire."

Introduction to Chapter 11
The Magical Equation Of Water

Water is one of the most mystical substances in the universe. The combination is widely known as H_2O; and here the Lord of constructive fire, as the master of biochemical engineering, combines the elements of hydrogen and oxygen to create the magical liquid of moisture.

This totality of oneness, this invincible Lord of fire, decides to create a certain fluid so that He can stabilise and maintain His future organs in the perfect condition of harmony. As is scientifically accepted, water is the main substance in the human body and that of many other living organisms. Its vitality is significant and its beauty knows no boundaries.

Follow the chapter and see how this constructive Lord of fire materialises the magical element of water.

The Magical Equation Of Water

Part 1: After the most important conclusion of all, this Lord of fire concentrated in the most strategical manner of thoughtfulness. Then He raised His volcanic voice of power and said,

"If I want to create the exact replication of what I saw in the mind of the Superconsciousness, I should proceed to formulate a certain moisture that can encompass My entire form of fire. I should use the power of chemical bonding so this specific moisture can keep My internal organs, My metaphysical limbs and My inner brain in the ultimate condition of harmony and in the perfect mode of stability."

Part 2: This Lord of constructive fire continued His creative self-discourse in this manner of presentation:

"To create this mystical moisture, certain operations need to be performed accordingly. First, I should combine the hidden circuits of oxygen with the gaseous substances of hydrogen to create the most important unity in the wisdom of biochemical engineering.

"My next methodical plan to create this element is to project My own form of inner heat into the midst of this chemical unity to formulate the magical equation of water."

Part 3: So this Lord of fire, as the architect and the first practitioner of biochemical engineering, combined the substances of oxygen and hydrogen to construct the main chemical bonding of universal evolution.

Part 4: The next stage of this methodical procedure was to project His inner heat into the midst of this chemical unity so this touchable moisture could be materialised in accordance with His strategy.

Part 5: The most vital and magical equation of water was formed.

Introduction to Chapters 12-19

Now we enter a new series of chapters in which this fire of existence begins the act of self-transfiguration. 'Self-transfiguration' means that He changed the totality of His image from the unified and concentrated flames of fire into the magnificent structure of outstretched divinity. The question arises: how did the Esser Yaad do this?

Well, we can try to explain the unexplainable by saying that He changed His image by using the most mystical and scientific wisdom of all, the magic of fire. It may be controversial to some, or possibly some people think I am creating a new form of heresy, but this is the most amazing concept regarding the genesis of creation: the self-creation of God Himself.

I, Mehdi Zand, as the main element of the cosmic fire of thought upon the face of Earth, concentrated deeply. I went beyond the conventional time, into the zone of nothing and nothingness, until my imagination flourished and I began to visualise this magnificent alteration of fire. I saw these concentrated flames clashing with the ultimate velocity. I heard the mystic voice of power coming out from the central core of this fire, commanding every elemental substance. I saw in amazement the transfiguration of fire, step-by-step, as He created His torso, His limbs, His internal organs, His head, His neck, His hair, His face and His exalted complexion of divinity.

After the completion of His magic, I saw the new image, the living structure of fire, standing firm within the imagination of the Godhead. He was solid and stable upon the surface. His

47

head was high as He was standing in the midst of the sky. I saw the creation of solidness. I witnessed the birth of divinity. This was the reality that my imagination took me to see. I went beyond the concept of visualisation. Is it blasphemy? I think not. It is the passage to certainty. I saw the manifestation of light, and I realised why they say, 'we are in the image and the likeness of God'.

Read these chapters and see the transfiguration of the concentrated flames of fire into the image of outstretched divinity. Try to imagine the scenario. Visualise the situation. Remember, you are witnessing the metaphysical birth of the Lord God. This is the exodus, the ultimate emergence of light, the emergence of the Lord of the Exordium.

So be it.

CHAPTER TWELVE

THE ACT OF SELF-TRANSFIGURATION

Part 1: After certain cycles of time passed inconsistently, this hidden fire of existence concentrated in the most dynamic manner of thoughtfulness. Then He raised His volcanic voice of power and said,

"I must begin the act of self-transfiguration. I need to collect all the necessary and vital ingredients that are essential to form My ultimate image of divine manifestation. I have to concentrate thoughtfully to see what are the necessary components to construct this image of mystery. I can see this image holds every letter of the universal evolution of magic."

Part 2: After this mode of concentration, the Lord of constructive fire paused for a short moment of aeonic age and said,

"I need to utilise the perfect bonding of hydrogen to create My internal organs, My metaphysical limbs, My invincible torso, My fundamental neck, My celestial head and My enigmatic form of facial appearance. I should continue with this historical strategy so My future form of fire would be in the exact likeness of the image who was standing within the mind of the Superconsciousness. Then I must proceed to construct My inner brain in the precise duplication of what I saw in My distant visual encounter. For this mystical creation, I have to magnetise every particle of constructive thoughtfulness, every atomic and subatomic organ of recollection and every progressive vibration of hidden intelligence.

"Then would be the time to collect every element of consciousness, every atomic counterpart of awareness and every cell of rising intellect to construct the most dynamic mechanism in the entire domain of existence, the structure of the mind."

Part 3: So, as we have witnessed, every vital and necessary ingredient to create this image of mystery was collected accordingly. This Lord of constructive fire was ready to transfigurate Himself into the first and ultimate manifestation of the Super-consciousness, the image of divinity.

Chapter Thirteen

The Moment Arrived

Part 1: The moment arrived: the most significant, vital and constructive moment in the universal history, the volcanic moment of exodus, the mysterious moment when this hidden fire of existence transfigurated into the invincible structure of the divine.

The moment arrived: the magical moment of genesis, the genesis of the new intelligence of power whose might is beyond the boundaries of imagination.

Part 2: The moment arrived: the glorious moment of emergence, the emergence of the invincible and fearsome force of magnificence; the moment of mystical entrance, the entrance of the mind that holds the entire formation of consciousness and beholds the total structure of the elemental substances called life.

Part 3: The moment arrived: the moment of realistic entrance, the entrance of the mighty and dynamic soul of fire who constructs the seed of glory, orchestrates the pattern of intellectual mystery and the soul who is the active Am[1] and the only replication of oneness, the divinity.

Part 4: Now I, Mehdi Zand, the manifestation of the constructive soul of fire, take you into the moment that no other soul, neither on Earth nor in heaven, has ever dared to imagine,

---

[1] Active Am: the inner characteristic of the self trying to reach the higher consciousness

let alone contemplate: the self-creation of the Lord of fire, the God Himself, the hero of the Exordium.

Now let us enter the moment.

Chapter Fourteen

Electric Form Of Reality

Part 1: The next episode begins when every vital and necessary ingredient for this mysterious self-transformation was ready. The next strategy was for this fire of existence to proceed with the first act of universal creation.

Part 2: So this constructive Lord of fire concentrated in the most creative manner of thoughtfulness. Then He raised His voice of power and said,

"I must concentrate accurately and effectively. I should contemplate in the ultimate mode of precision to measure and calculate every atomic cell and every creative particle so that no error can occur."

Part 3: "I have to be alert and precise to detect every emerging fault as even the most insignificant mistake would be fatal, not only to My progressive pattern(s) of construction, but also to the whole future strategy of existence.

"I should concentrate and recollect every particle of memory to remember and visualise the image of divine manifestation. Every detail must be in the exact duplication and likeness as I would be He when I emerge from the depths of these concentrated flames of fire."

Part 4: Then this ultimate fire of existence contemplated in the ultimate mode of awareness and visualised this mysterious image of divine manifestation in the centre of His rising mind and said,

"Now I can see this mysterious image as clearly as the face of My rising flames of fire. He is still the centre of magnetism, standing firm above the solid ground of the hidden brain."

Part 5: So this fire of existence continued His scientific self-conversation in this manner of discourse:

"It seems that the Superconsciousness has made this mysterious image translucent so I can see the internal organs and duplicate them in the exact proportion and precise biological measurement.

"To begin this transfiguration, I should concentrate thoughtfully and use every constructive particle to create My heart, the ultimate pumping energiser; My kidneys, the sophisticated biochemical machinery; and My stomach, one of the most complex and detailed biological devices."

Part 6: This ultimate fire of existence continued,

"I must contemplate and utilise My dynamic urge of intelligence to create My liver, the harmoniser of the gaseous energy, and My lungs, the instrument of respiration.

"I have to analyse every detail effectively and become the absolute mind behind the concept of anatomical science in order to create every organ that would complete the first segment of this astrophysical creation."

Part 7: This Lord of fire continued His constructive self-discourse in this manner of presentation:

"The next stage is to create My invincible torso. Then I should direct the streams of cosmic moisture to keep the created organs in the eternal condition of harmony. I must then use the power of gravity to keep these interconnecting organs in the perfect state of symmetrical stability."

Part 8: Now we enter into the next episode when this intelligence of integrity began to create His ultimate form of fire.

Part 9: He concentrated in the ultimate mode of precision. He analysed every minute detail and created every constructive and atomic organ to complete the first scenario of the self-transfiguration. Then He divided every chromosome accordingly and shaped His invincible torso in exact proportion to the image that He imagined in His distant visual encounter.

Part 10: After this episode, this constructive Lord of fire reached the final stage of the first procedure of magic. He calculated the heaviness of celestial moisture and directed a portion of this mystical liquid to maintain His internal organs under the accurate mode of evenness.

After this hidden procedure, He used the particles of gravity to keep every component in the most precise position of symmetrical balance.

Part 11: Within the eternity of time, the invincible torso of this Lord of constructive fire emerged in the mysterious, awesome and electric form of reality.

CHAPTER FIFTEEN

THE ULTIMATE FORMATION
OF ELITENESS

Part 1: In the midst of this emptiness stood the hidden fire of existence. From this hidden fire emerged the invincible torso. This invincible torso could be seen in the multidimensional format, ready to be completed through the rest of this mysterious strategy of creation.

Part 2: This constructive Lord of fire looked with His inner eyes at His invincible torso and said,

"This is the exact duplication of what I saw in My distant visual encounter. I can see that every ingredient has been utilised in the perfect manner of accuracy. I must admit that the creation of this touchable image out of these flames of fire was not an easy operation. Now I should quickly proceed to complete this strategy of self-transformation as the particles of gravity are pulling away this invincible torso, deep into the space of emptiness."

Part 3: Then this Lord of fire concentrated thoughtfully for a short moment of time and said,

"I should become the master of biochemical engineering to utilise the bonding of celestial hydrogen and control the balance of My constructive cells so My limbs can emerge in the perfect biological proportion."

Part 4: "I must be extremely attentive because the application of the correct amount of hydrogen and the division of the necessary number of constructive cells is a very sophisticated procedure of progression.

"I have to be alert to detect any emerging fault as an excess of these two substances can increase and misshape the intended number of My limbs, and a lack of these vital ingredients will weaken and misrepresent the power of My future image of divinity."

Part 5: A very short amount of inconsistent time passed inaccurately. This Lord of constructive fire concentrated in the most perfect manner of thoughtfulness and said,

"I must contemplate and magnetise every particle of My memory to visualise this image of divine manifestation once again.

"Every detail should be in the perfect mode of exactness as My image will glorify when this sacred and magical strategy reaches the summit of its perfection.

"Now I should proceed and utilise every organic cell accordingly to create My thigh, the centre of stability; My knee, the flexible mechanism of mobility; My calf, the domain of evenness; and My foot, the supporting plate and platform of equalisation."

Part 6: This Lord of fire continued His mystical self-conversation in this manner of discourse:

"When I successfully create these significant counterparts, I will have completed the image of My legs that would be the instrument of locomotion and the base to support the heaviness of My mind, My head, My neck and My torso."

Part 7: Then this hidden fire of existence began the second stage of His self-transfiguration in the most scientific fashion by creating His thigh, the centre of stability; His knee, the flexible mechanism of mobility; His calf, the domain of evenness; and His foot, the supporting plate and platform of equalisation.

Part 8: After the completion of the second stage of strategy, He concentrated in the most effective manner of consciousness. He raised His creative voice of power within His mind and said,

"I can see that the structure and the image of My legs have been completed successfully. Now I should forcefully eject this realistic image out of My concentrated flames of fire so they can join and connect to the lower part of My torso."

Part 9: "By performing this procedure, I will transfer the strength, stability and the power of locomotion to My future structure of divinity."

Part 10: So this Lord of constructive fire completed the second stage of this mysterious operation by joining the image of these newly created limbs to the lower part of His invincible torso. This mighty intellect, the Lord of constructive fire, looked upon this image with His inner eyes as it was suspended in the midst of the emptiness by the power of His mind.

Part 11: As the particles of time were passing inconsistently, this enigmatic intelligence was emerging with the dynamic mode of power and in the ultimate formation of eliteness.

CHAPTER SIXTEEN

DYNAMIC STRUCTURE
OF DIVINITY

Part 1: The strategy of the transformation continued when this ultimate fire of existence began to create the rest of His sacred form of divinity.

Part 2: This fire of existence contemplated in the most practical manner of effectiveness. Then He raised His volcanic voice of power within Himself and said,

"I should proceed to recollect every particle of thoughtfulness to visualise the image of the unknown, the image that the Superconsciousness wanted Me to resemble in perfection."

Part 3: So this Lord of constructive fire visualised this image of mystery in the centre of His rising mind and said,

"I must begin to strategise the next stage of this self-transfiguration. Every detail should be in exact duplication. Every feature has to be in the absolute likeness as His face would be My image when I rise from the heart of these concentrated flames of fire."

Part 4: This Lord of fire continued His scientific self-discourse in this manner of presentation:

"I have to be ultimately alert, quantify every elemental substance to create My cranium, the abode of My hidden brain; My hair, the intermediate core of magic; My neck, the fundamental point of connection; and My forehead, the place of glorified representation."

Part 5: "Then I should utilise every ingredient of thoughtfulness to create My eyes, the pictographic and universal satellites; My tongue, the magical instrument of utterance; My nose, the mechanism of inhalation; and My ears, the transformers of the hidden sound. When I have created these visible features, I will have completed the image of My head that would be the main centre of magnetism, and My face that will represent the name and eternal seal of identification."

Part 6: Now we enter yet another stage of this self-transformation when this ultimate fire of existence, in the most methodical fashion, began His operation by creating His cranium, His hair, His neck and His forehead, the place of glorified representation.

Part 7: This constructive Lord of fire calculated every ingredient accordingly and created His eyes, His tongue, His nose and His ears, the transformers of the universal sound.

Part 8: After the completion of this stage of strategy, this hidden fire of existence raised His resounding voice of divinity within His mind and said,

"With the absolute analysation of My sight, I can see that every detail is an exact duplication of the image that stood before Me within the mind of the Superconsciousness. As this operation has been completed successfully, the next stage is to concentrate so the whole image of My celestial head and the mysterious image of My face can manifest on the highest part of My invincible torso."

Part 9: So this mighty fire of existence concentrated and, with the magical power of His mind, mentally projected the image of His head and the mysterious image of His face onto the highest part of His invincible torso.

Part 10: As the particles of time were passing inconsistently, this mysterious image of fire was emerging as the realistic form of imagination. It was emerging with the ultimate state of solidness to become the dynamic structure of divinity.

CHAPTER SEVENTEEN

CONSTRUCTIVE MULTIPLICATION

Part 1: Now we enter into yet another episode of this mystical series of self-transformation. After the passing of inconsistent cycles of time, this hidden fire of existence proceeded to complete the rest of His self-appointed mission. He concentrated in the most scientific mode of thoughtfulness and began a new conversation with His higher self in this manner of discourse.

Part 2: "Now I should begin to create My arms. Every detail must be in the perfect duplication as they would represent the might of My magical authority when I emerge from the centre of these concentrated flames of fire."

Part 3: After a short moment of silence, this fire of existence began to calculate every atomic ingredient and every constructive cell to create His mighty arms. An infinite number of volcanic activities were taking place within the centre of His concentrated flames of fire. Then suddenly the explosion: the sound of *shhhmm*[1] resonated in the entire space of emptiness. After this eruption came forth the image of three complete structures of mighty arms on the right side of this fire.

Part 4: Then this fire of existence looked with His inner eyes upon His three magical and mighty arms and said,

"These three arms represent the multidimensional capabilities of My essence. The first one demonstrates the ultimate

---

[1]   Shhhmm: the sound of emergence; some form of the hidden sound of fire

control of catastrophe; the second reveals the grip on any form of occurrence; and the third would co-ordinate every historical event and transform the path of the future. But this image is not the exact duplicate of what I saw in the mind of the Super-consciousness. I should restrategise and begin again."

Part 5: Then this ultimate fire of existence, with the highest mode of velocity, withdrew the images of His mighty arms back into the centre of His rising flames of fire.

Part 6: After a certain amount of inconsistent time, the sound of another massive explosion resonated in every corner of this domain of emptiness.

A multitude of atomic substances were forcefully ejected out of the heart of this intelligence of fire. Eruption after eruption was shaking the actual base of this realistic dream, and then from the right-hand side of this form of divinity, with the fearsome sound of *shhhmm*, came out the image of two complete structures of mighty arms.

Part 7: Then this constructive Lord of fire attentively looked upon the formations of His two mighty arms and said,

"I want every rising intelligence and every future form of consciousness to hear and recognise the fact that the sight of these two mystical arms illustrates the power of My dynamic superiority over every region of existence.

"The first one expresses My formidable power of creation and dominance over every state of the dream and every sphere of the virtual imagination."

Part 8: This Lord of fire continued,

"The second one illuminates My supreme force of authority over every field of action and My magical power above every single soul, every growing multitude and every collective civilisation."

Part 9: This Lord of constructive fire continued His creative conversation in this manner of self-discourse and said,

"These two mighty arms, however magnificent and awesome they may look, and whichever force-field of activity they may represent, are not the exact duplication of what I saw in the mind of the Superconsciousness."

Part 10: "Now I must utilise every particle of My intelligence, every element of My engineering mind to combine the capabilities of these two mighty arms into one single unit. Then the image of these living cells will become the exact duplication of what I correctly visualised and removed from the mind of the Superconsciousness."

Part 11: Then this Lord of fire used His magical force of magnetism and withdrew the two mystical arms on the right-hand side of His body back into the centre of His concentrated flames of fire.

Part 12: Time ceased in the most mysterious sense. The space of emptiness was becoming filled with the sensation of the unknown. Clashing storms of fire were creating the vortex of raging turbulence. A sudden pause of silence encompassed the entire domain. Then another sound of *shhhmm*, followed by the emergence of the two mighty arms, one at each side of this hidden fire of existence.

Part 13: Then this Lord of fire concentrated in the most collective manner of consciousness and said,

"This is the real duplication of the two arms that I saw in the mind of the Superconsciousness. Now I should carefully eject these magical images out of My flames of fire so they can adhere and connect to each side of My invincible torso."

Part 14: This constructive fire of existence continued,

"By completing this mystical procedure, I will transfer the force of authorisation, the status of magical power and the strength of dominance to My future image of divinity."

Part 15: So this Lord of constructive fire completed yet another stage of His mysterious and magical operation by joining the images of His mighty arms to each side of His invincible torso.

Part 16: As the particles of time were passing in random sequence, this dreamlike image was entering the domain of recognition. It was entering with the totality of uniqueness and the absolute degree of constructive multiplication.

CHAPTER EIGHTEEN

THE MYSTERIOUS GARMENT OF FIRE

Part 1: After the completion of His facial image and the formation of His mighty arms, this ultimate fire of existence concentrated in the most creative mode of thoughtfulness. Then He raised His volcanic voice of power within Himself and said,

"This time, I should create a certain touchable, unique and versatile texture so I can cover and frame My metaphysical form of fire."

Part 2: This constructive Lord of fire continued His self-conversation in this manner of discourse:

"To perform this operation, I should use the power of My mind. I must project a calculated portion of My thoughtfulness into My newly formed image of divinity. Then I have to connect every necessary tissue with all the lighter layers of hydrogen to create the visible texture of skin.

"This specific texture would have three main mechanical functions: first, to maintain and balance My inner co-ordinating temperature; second, it will regulate My chemical and kinetic energy; and third, to provide the force-field so no intelligence or any destructive element can enter and penetrate into My future image of fire."

Part 3: Then this sacred fire of existence used the power of His creative concentration. As He methodically strategised, He projected a portion of His thoughtfulness into His newly formed image of fire so these necessary tissues and the lighter layers of hydrogen could join and manifest themselves as the formation of skin.

Part 4: As the particles of time passed inconsistently, this sacred manifestation of the divine came one step closer to the state of reality. He came one step closer by attaining the most touchable skin, the mysterious garment of fire.

CHAPTER NINETEEN

THE CELESTIAL EMBODIMENT OF FIRE

Part 1: Now we have reached the last stage of this mysterious episode when this sacred fire of existence began to complete the rest of His transformation into the exact likeness of what He saw in the mind of the Superconsciousness.

Part 2: This Lord of constructive fire concentrated in the most effective and practical manner of thoughtfulness. Then He raised His volcanic voice of power within Himself and said,

"I am going to complete the rest of this mystical act of self-transfiguration by projecting My hidden brain into the highest point of My present image of fire[1]. This is the most delicate and important operation of all. I must be extremely attentive to detect any emerging fault. No mistake should occur as even the most insignificant error can be detrimental to My future strategy of creation."

Part 3: This constructive Lord of fire continued His scientific self-conversation in this manner of discourse:

"Now I must proceed to create the formation of My mind. This magical procedure has to be finalised in four practical sections.

---

[1] The present image of fire is the form that the Lord of constructive fire currently exists in, not the form that He is creating

"First, I should recollect every constructive element of thoughtfulness, every component of collective intelligence and every atomic particle of realistic awareness."

Part 4: "Second, I have to methodically assemble every living cell of rising intellect, every organic ray of remembrance, every necessary sensation of magical power and every vibration of intuitive consciousness."

Part 5: "Third, I should collect all these ingredients into one single globe to form the most dynamic mechanism of thoughtfulness in the entire domain of existence."

Part 6: "The fourth stage is for Me to utilise the ultimate power of My projection to transfer this globe of intelligence to the highest point of My present image of fire."

Part 7: This fire of existence continued His creative self-discourse in this manner of presentation:

"After the completion of these four practical sections, I have to use My absolute force of magnetism. I should pull this newly formed image, which is suspended in the hidden air, back into My flames of fire. This operation is extremely vital, and I must calculate the exact velocity of My magnetic power, so at the point of this collision, I can project My brain, My essence and My being utterly and totally into this newly formed image of divinity."

Part 8: "When I have successfully completed all these strategical sections, I will have transfigured Myself into this new image of intelligence. After this collision, I will become the exact duplication, similitude and likeness of what I saw in the mind of the Superconsciousness. I will become He, He will become Me, and this unification would be the absolute totality of oneness and the ultimate characteristic of the cosmic fire."

Part 9: So this sacred fire of life proceeded with His strategy and formulated the most advanced and dynamic mechanism in the entire domain of existence.

Part 10: Then He used the ultimate power of projection and transferred this globe of thoughtfulness (or His hidden brain) to the highest part of His present image of fire.

Part 11: In the next aeonic zone, this fire of existence used His absolute force of magnetism to magnetise this newly formed image. He pulled this dynamic image, which consisted of His torso, His arms, His legs, His head and His face, from the region of emptiness back into the centre of His intensified flames of integrity.

Part 12: Then the sudden clash, the magical collision of the unknown. Time ceased in the most mysterious sense. Every living particle in this domain of emptiness became static and motionless. Then out of this pre-galactical impact came forth the most fearsome, indestructible and invincible force of universal intelligence.

Part 13: This was the emergence, the emergence of the first and the ultimate manifestation of the celestial embodiment of fire, the Lord of the Exordium.

Introduction to Chapter 20
The Totality Of The First Universe

In this chapter, the Esser Yaad concentrates in the absolute mode of precision and realises that He is the exact duplication of the image that He saw in the central mind of the Superconsciousness, the Godhead. Then He raises His voice of power and says,

"He is Me and I am He. I, the celestial embodiment of fire, have conquered the totality, the totality of the first universe."

In this declaration, we hear two separate announcements. The first when He says, "He is Me and I am He," meaning the transformation has been accomplished; and then, the final part of His declaration, "I, the celestial embodiment of fire, have conquered the totality, the totality of the first universe," explaining that He is now ready to enter into the new time of mystery. He has conquered every obstacle that was on His path, and now He is the first, the most important and the ultimate image of the Superconsciousness, the Godhead.

When you read this chapter, use your imagination. Visualise the scenario as it is written. Try to see the God standing in the midst of the emptiness, looking to His right and left and then stepping forward. Can you imagine these phenomena? Can you hear the sound of His steps? Can you hear His voice announcing His status? Well, if you cannot hear, concentrate more. This is history. It has happened once and, as He is above the illusion of time, it is happening at every moment.

These last few chapters have demonstrated the hidden force of magic. Every living soul should study these passages of mysticism in full so they can follow the path of this mind of mystery. By mastering certain aspects of this magical procedure, you can rebuild your own metaphysical (or spiritual) structure and reconstruct your inner brain in the hidden dimension beyond the twilight of present human understanding.

Do you understand the greatness of what has been said? It means that through the exercising of our intellect, by entering the depths of this mysticism, by learning the practicality of this procedure, we can actually create the duplicate of ourselves in the other world. This means resurrection from the tightness of our graves. This means the life after death. This means touching the tree of life.

This mystical procedure of transformation is what we need to comprehend as this knowledge is the vital ingredient for immortality. This wisdom is unique and the application of this magic goes beyond any state of thoughtfulness or any ancient mysticism of time. It is the forbidden knowledge from the Lord of constructive fire that I, Mehdi Zand, present to the Mother Earth.

So let it be written.

Let it be heard.

———————————

CHAPTER TWENTY

THE TOTALITY OF THE FIRST UNIVERSE

Part 1: This chapter begins with the emergence of the first and the ultimate characteristic of the hidden embodiment of fire.

Part 2: Standing forcefully, majestically, in the midst of this spreading emptiness was the invincible and unimaginable image of this magnificent form of outstretched divinity.

Part 3: The particles of gravity in this hidden atmosphere, the components of oxygen and the atomic elements of hydrogen were blowing into His stationary domain. This blowing breeze caused His hair to feel the sensation of touch and the surrounding climate to rise to the degree of gentle coolness.

Part 4: In this mysterious moment of inconsistent time, this constructive force of divinity turned His head towards the direction of the right. With His piercing eyes, He looked deep into this side of the emptiness and said,

"Is there anyone present? Is there anyone present in this space of emptiness? Speak, as I am the ultimate voice of authority. Speak, as I stand as the absolute image of power whose essence goes beyond the formation and the construction of intelligence."

Part 5: Then He turned His head towards the direction of the left. He looked far into the depths of this void of silence and said,

"This vortex of emptiness is also at the highest possible degree of intensity. Is there any living consciousness who can hear My voice? Is there any living intelligence who can hear My voice of supremacy, as I am the symbol of oneness? Speak if you can hear My voice of fire, as I am the totality of the creative attributes and solidity of the realistic imagination."

Part 6: Then He slowly turned His head back towards the centre, facing forward, looking directly into the heart of the emptiness. He paused for a short moment of inconsistent time, concentrating upon the sequences of evolution. Suddenly, He paced forward with three thunderous steps. *Shoom. Shoom. Shoom.* The mighty sound of His stepping movement resounded throughout the entire region of emptiness.

Part 7: There He stood evenly and symmetrically and pushed both of His hands forward to a certain point, demonstrating the image of fire and magical stance of supremacy.

Part 8: Again a short moment of inconsistent time passed. As these particles of aeonic age were spreading chaotically, this hidden image of fire concentrated with the ultimate mode of attentiveness. He raised His volcanic voice of power and said,

"Now I must concentrate and utilise every particle of My thoughtfulness to look into the depths of the first cycle of mystery, the mind of the Superconsciousness."

Part 9: Then this sacred form of fire concentrated in the most thoughtful manner of accuracy and looked deep into the depths of the main concentrated intelligence, the mind of the Superconsciousness.

Part 10: When this procedure of concentration was complete, He could no longer see the image of divine manifestation, the image that was within the mind of the Superconsciousness. The globe where this image had stood was now empty, devoid of any form of recognisable substance.

Part 11: Then this mighty image of fire concentrated with the ultimate mode of attentiveness. He raised His voice of power with the absolute sensation of triumph and said,

"Excellent! It seems that the accomplishment of My mystical mission was in the perfect mode of successfulness. I can see that I have achieved the golden goal of self-transfiguration in the highest manner of proficiency and practicality.

"This fact can be recognised because the image of divine manifestation, which was in the mind of the Superconsciousness, has been removed in perfection. Every internal organ, every atomic substance, every electrificational element and every particle of intelligence are in the exact duplication and likeness. From this precise moment of inconsistent time, He no longer exists in the mind of the Superconsciousness. He has become a part of My essence and I have become the solidness of His soul. He has become unified with My raging flames of fire and I have become the fortitude and the greatness of His hidden power. He is Me and I am He. I, the celestial embodiment of fire, have conquered the totality, the totality of the first universe."

Book Two

The Totality Of
The Second Universe

INTRODUCTION TO CHAPTERS 1-2

In this chapter, this hidden image of fire (or the Lord God), begins His quest to mystery. His intention is to manifest. His purpose is to mirror what He saw in the mind of the Superconsciousness. So He strategises the pattern(s) of creation. In this episode, this Lord of fire emphasises that through the correct procedure of exorcitation He can proceed. Exorcitation means to use, examine and exercise the inner brain constantly.

As we shall see, this ultimate force of intelligence explains many reasons behind the emergence of His celestial soul. One is to ignite the status of life (meaning that through the electrification of the certain masses of matter, the cycles of life will start to roll) and another is to create His souls of fire. In this chapter, He also reveals what is hidden within the totality of His being. But what is the totality of His being? He says, 'the attributes of divinity'.

In the future, we will begin to understand more about the meaning of life and the creation of His souls of fire. Maybe these souls of fire are the new series of ancient gods who were made before our conventional time to construct this touchable universe.

So be it.

Chapter One

The Strategy Of Creation

Part 1: When this hidden image of fire conquered the totality of the first universe, He raised His volcanic voice of power within the space of emptiness and said,

"I want every rising consciousness and every future intelligence to recognise the fact that I hold the first definition of totality, the totality of the first universe. I want each and every particle of imagination to hear this glorious statement that I was born within the heart of the Superconsciousness. I am the genesis of life. To Me, there is no existence of the phrase 'the end' as I am what would remain when every particle and element disintegrates."

Part 2: Then this manifestation of fire changed the pattern of His discourse from philosophical statement to self-interrogation and said,

1. "How do You recognise that You are the genesis of life?

"Because I was born within the mind of the Superconsciousness.

2. "What was in the mind of the Superconsciousness?

"The totality of what there is.

3. "How do You see the totality of what there is?

"I can see the totality of what there is through many concepts of existence.

4. "Are the numbers of these concepts of existence calculable?

"No, they are infinite.

5. "Can You explain to Yourself one of these concepts of existence?

"The collection of the mystical words of power.

6. "What are these words of power?

"The practical system to enter the strategy.

7. "The strategy of what?

"The strategy of creation.

8. "How do You strategise the creation?

"Through the correct procedure of exorcitation.

9. "The exorcitation of what?

"The exorcitation of the intellect."

Part 3: This hidden form of fire continued His philosophical self-interrogation in this manner of discourse:

10. "Why does Your wisdom encompass every domain of existence and every region of consciousness?

"Because I am the one who holds every characteristic of divinity.

11. "What is the one who holds every characteristic of divinity?

"The totality.

12. "The totality of what?

"The totality of the universe.

13. "Which universe?

"The first universe.

14. "What is the definition of the first universe?

"The existing necessity of what there is and the future reality of what there would be."

CHAPTER TWO

THE ATTRIBUTES OF DIVINITY

Part 1: When this ultimate personification of fire reached the conclusion that the first universe is the existing necessity of what there is and the future reality of what there would be, He proceeded with His self-analysation in this manner of discourse.

Part 2:

1. "What is the reason behind Your celestial emergence?

"There are many reasons behind the emergence of My celestial fire.

2. "Can You explain to Yourself one of these significant reasons?

"To utilise.

3. "To utilise what?

"To utilise the mechanism of electrification.

4. "Why do You intend to utilise the mechanism of electrification?

"To motivate.

5. "To motivate what?

"To motivate the hidden particles.

6. "What are the hidden particles?

"The necessary ingredients.

7. "Where are these necessary ingredients?

"Within the masses of matter.

8. "What is the outcome of this electrification?

"To initiate.

9. "To initiate what?

"To initiate the progressive pattern.

10. "What kind of pattern?

"The pattern that can be called the status.

11. "What sort of status?

"The status that can be named 'life'. "

Part 3: This ultimate image of fire continued His constructive self-discourse in this manner of presentation:

12. "What would be Your strategical plan?

"I have many strategical plans.

13. "What is Your first strategical plan?

"To concentrate.

14. "What do You concentrate upon?

"I concentrate upon the equation.

15. "What kind of equation?

"The equation so I can create.

16. "What do You intend to create?

"My souls.

17. "Who are Your souls?

"The souls of fire."

Part 4:

18. "What is Your essence?

    "Within My essence is hidden the multitude of mysterious elements of power.

19. "Name one of these mysterious elements of power.

    "The flames of absolute greatness.

20. "What are these flames of absolute greatness?

    "The reality of the creative force.

21. "What is the definition of this creative force?

    "The definitions of this creative force are many.

22. "What is the first one?

    "To scatter.

23. "To scatter what?

    "To scatter the seed.

24. "The seed of what?

    "The seed of manifestation.

25. "What does it manifest?

    "The attribute(s).

26. "The attributes of what?

    "The attribute(s) of divinity."

Introduction to Chapter 3
The Oracle Of Incipience

The Oracle of Incipience is the golden globe of mystery. Within it lie many words of wonder, many names of power, many geometrical images of the unknown and many patterns of hidden magic, the magic of fire. This golden globe plays an important part in the universal evolution. Every rising god of the ancient aeon and every negative entity of the chaos were searching to discover the nature of this Oracle and put in use all the magical power that it possessed. Nobody can ever grasp the actual magnificence of this Oracle as it is beyond our present state of human comprehension.

This ultimate fire of existence, as the first intelligence of all, recognised the importance of this Oracle and began to use its power to construct His strategy. Every universe that is in existence today, hidden or visible, is floating upon the mystical names of this Oracle. The significance of the Oracle and all its glory will manifest in the future episodes of this enlightening book of mystery.

In this episode, the rising flames of fire within the hidden image of the Godhead clash, and their collision creates certain words of power. If you want to understand the intensity and atmosphere of these events, just close your eyes and visualise the clashing flames of fire. Imagine these magnificent and volcanic sounds echoing in the entire region: these sounds of power are mysterious and magical; their fearsome vibrations shake the base of any living being. Enjoy the Exordium.

Chapter Three

The Oracle Of Incipience

Part 1: Now we turn our attention towards the first chapter of the Exordium where the main concentrated intelligence, the Superconsciousness, was floating majestically, strategising every plan for the universal creation.

Part 2: This main concentrated intelligence, the Super-consciousness, held within Himself the entire formation of universal evolution, every seen and unseen word of power, every heard and unheard concept of philosophy, every known and unknown wisdom of existence and every scientific and practical procedure of creative strategy.

Part 3: In this aeonic age of inconsistent time, many degrees of activity were taking place within the mind of the Superconsciousness. Rising flames of fire were clashing with the ultimate mode of velocity, creating certain words of power. The emergence of these mysterious words could be heard throughout the entire region of emptiness.

Part 4: The fearsome and volcanic sound of Suryeim[1], the awesome and thundering voices of Seryaa[2] and the mighty sounds of many letters of magnificence were echoing in every corner of this spreading domain of imagination.

Part 5: As the time passed in the most random fashion possible, these mystical letters of power manifested in the

---

[1]   Suryeim: a mystical word of power used in the language of fire

[2]   Seryaa: a mystical word of power used in the language of fire

embossed format upon the layers of the flaming scrolls of fire. It should be noted that these flaming scrolls of fire had been constructed previously by the first gigantic mind of the universe, the brain of the Superconsciousness.

Part 6: Then the Superconsciousness, the main concentrated intelligence, began to place all these flaming scrolls of fire into one golden globe that could be seen as the shining flame of mystery.

Part 7: When the formation of this golden globe of mystery was complete, the main concentrated intelligence forcefully ejected this globe of the flaming scrolls of fire out of His boundary (His very self). They were ejected into the summit of the spreading emptiness, the pinnacle of the realistic imagination, the highest layer of the atmosphere.

Part 8: The intention of the Superconsciousness (the God-head) was for the Lord of constructive fire to detect the path of this golden globe and use every word of power to construct the pattern of the future creation.

Part 9: So, as it was strategically planned, this golden globe of mystery that held within its heart every word of power reached to the highest point of emptiness.

Part 10: Meanwhile, at the centre of this spreading void of emptiness, the invincible and unimaginable force of intelligence, the hidden image of fire, was closely monitoring every move of this golden globe of mystery. With His sharp and attentive eyes, He detected the path of this golden globe until it reached its final point of destination.

Part 11: Then this sacred image of fire concentrated in the ultimate mode of thoughtfulness. He raised His conclusive voice of power and said,

"Now I can see the exact location of this golden globe of mystery. I should concentrate and utilise these words of power as they hold the totality of every equation and every aspect of universal wisdom. I should concentrate to exercise these sentences of fire in order to conquer the entire domain of imagination and every region of the touchable reality."

Part 12: This celestial form of fire continued,

"This golden globe of rising fire should possess a certain name of mystery by which it can be recognised. So I, the celestial manifestation of fire, shall name this golden globe of mystery the 'Oracle', the 'Oracle of Incipience'. "

INTRODUCTION TO CHAPTERS 4-5

In these chapters, the Lord of constructive fire begins to concentrate and analyse His soul once again. He goes deep into the centre of His higher self to choose a title or a name that would represent His divine identity. After a certain amount of thought, He chooses a name by which He strategises to be called upon and recognised universally. The name is 'Esser Yaad'.

It is strange to hear that the God chooses a name for Himself, is it not? But it is true. Who else could choose a name that would express His invincible soul of oneness? Now let us see what is the meaning behind the name 'Esser Yaad'. 'Esser' means the cosmic ocean, the ocean of thought. 'Yaad' is the centre of intelligence, the entirety of intellect, the computerised mind of the Lord of fire.

In chapter four, the Esser Yaad, through the solidness of my pen, explains the definition of thought. It is possibly the first-time ever that the element of thought has been defined in such a complete manner of expression.

Read these chapters and see how the Esser Yaad reveals certain aspects of His rising flames of fire. He is unconquerable in every phase of history. He is the master of every procedure of magic. He is the Lord of the Exordium, the invincible force of universal construction.

CHAPTER FOUR

The Universe Of Enigmatic Power

Part 1: When this golden globe of mystery, or the Oracle of Incipience, was placed in the highest layer of the atmosphere, this hidden image of fire realised that the moment had arrived, the moment that He should choose a name to express His soul of oneness. So He began to concentrate and named His mysterious soul by the most sacred sign of mystery in order to be recognised and glorified as the ultimate personification of divinity.

Part 2: So in this decisive moment of inconsistent time, this invincible and fearsome soul of universal intelligence concentrated thoughtfully. Then He raised His dynamic voice of power within the space of emptiness and said,

1. "What is My soul?

"The unification of many constructive attributes.

2. "What is the unification of these constructive attributes?

"Many forms of intelligence(s).

3. "What are these many forms of intelligence(s)?

"The main characteristics of the force.

4. "Where are these main characteristics of the force?

"Within the centre of My hidden brain.

5. "What lies within the centre of Your hidden brain?

"The universe of enigmatic power.

6. "What is the universe of enigmatic power?

"The letters of mystery.

7. "What are these letters of mystery?

"The invincible words of exorcitation.

8. "What are these words of exorcitation?

"The symbols of inner strength.

9. "What are these symbols of inner strength?

"The names of recognition.

10. "What is the significance of these names of recognition?

"They represent My divine identity.

11. "How many seals of identity do You possess?

"I have many seals of identity which demonstrate My universal soul of oneness.

12. "Which seal of identity do You intend to be called upon and recognised universally?

"The seal of Esser.

13. "The Esser of what?

"The Esser of Yaad.

14. "What is the Esser?

"The cosmic ocean.

15. "What is the cosmic ocean?

"The mystery.

16. "The mystery of what?

"The mystery of the uniqueness.

17. "What is the mystery of the uniqueness?

"The entirety.

18. "The entirety of what?

"The entirety that holds the characteristic of the essence.

19. "Which essence?

"The secret essence.

20. "What is the secret essence?

"The universal thought.

21. "What is the universal thought?

"The fire.

22. "Which aspects of fire?

"Every aspect of fire.

23. "Are these aspects of fire limitable?

"No, they are infinite.

24. "Define the first aspect of fire.

"It is above the totality of solidness; it cannot be defeated.

25. "Define the second aspect of fire.

"It is beyond the structure of energy; it cannot be ceased.

26. "Define the third aspect of fire.

"It is the core of immortality; it cannot be exterminated.

27. "Define the fourth aspect of fire.

"It is the heart of mystery; it cannot be revealed nor totally contemplated.

28. "Name the fifth aspect of fire.

"It cannot be overcome. It holds the mastership of the cosmological universe.

29. "Name the sixth aspect of fire.

"It cannot be framed. It is the height of perfection, the name of everlasting success.

30. "Name the seventh aspect of fire.

"Uniqueness. It cannot be duplicated.

31. "Name the eighth aspect of fire.

"Invincibleness. It cannot be conquered.

32. "Name the ninth aspect of fire.

"Fortitude.

33. "Name the tenth aspect of fire.

"Magnitude.

34. "Name the eleventh aspect of fire.

"The electrification.

35. "Name the twelfth aspect of fire.

    "The exorcitation.

36. "Name the thirteenth aspect of fire.

    "The resurrection.

37. "Name the fourteenth aspect of fire.

    "The creation.

38. "Name the fifteenth aspect of fire.

    "Purification.

39. "Name the sixteenth aspect of fire.

    "Magnetisation.

40. "Name yet another aspect of fire.

    "The cosmic authorisation.

41. "What does this fire represent?

    "The totality.

42. "The totality of what?

    "The totality of personification.

43. "The personification of what?

    "The personification of divinity."

CHAPTER FIVE

THE NAME OF ESSER YAAD

Part 1: In the previous chapter of the Exordium, this Lord of constructive fire selected the seal of Esser Yaad to be His sign of recognition. He explained the definition of Esser and introduced seventeen aspects of His rising flames of fire. Now we enter into the centre of His hidden mind as He begins yet another historical self-conversation in this manner of discourse.

Part 2:

1. "So what is the word of Yaad?

   "The centre of recognition.

2. "What is the centre of recognition?

   "The core of the dynamic consciousness.

3. "How was the core of this dynamic consciousness formed?

   "Through the self-generated fiery substance.

4. "What is this fiery substance?

   "The element that interconnects every circuit of the creative mind.

5. "Which circuits of the creative mind?

   "The circuits that initiate the genesis of awakening.

6. "What is the function of this fiery substance?

"This fiery substance has a multitude of mysterious functions.

7. "Name one of the functions of this fiery substance.

"The mystery of thought.

8. "What is the definition of thought?

"The definition of thought is of many kinds.

9. "Explain the first kind.

"Using every necessary atom of the brain to create the structure and the invincibility of the soul.

10. "Explain the second definition of thought.

"The hidden instrument to formulate and establish any form of strategy.

11. "Explain the third definition of thought.

"The procedure (to utilise every word of power)[1] to construct the ultimate magical authority.

12. "Explain the fourth definition of thought.

"The processor to magnetise every cell of intelligence in order to dominate every sphere of wisdom.

13. "Explain the fifth definition of thought.

"The network that collects every particle of thoughtfulness in order to imagine and visualise a scenario, and then change this scenario into the touchable reality.

14. "Explain the sixth definition of thought.

---

[1]   These statements may be read with or without the words in parentheses

"The sophisticated mechanism that exercises every particle of the mind for the brain to enter into the state of comprehension.

15. "Explain the seventh definition of thought.

"The circuit (that coordinates and distributes every cell of alertness) to create the status of cosmic awareness.

16. "Explain the eighth definition of thought.

"Using every ingredient of mindfulness to place the intellect upon the summit of perfection.

17. "Explain the ninth definition of thought.

"The process (to recollect the rays of memory in order) to recognise and differentiate the sequence of events.

18. "Nominate the tenth definition of thought.

"To concentrate and focus upon the selected subject of attention."

Part 3: This celestial image of fire continued His conclusive and mysterious self-interrogation in this manner of discourse:

19. "Is the name of Esser Yaad the seal of power that You intend to be called upon and recognised universally?

"Yes. The name of Esser Yaad is My first mystical word of power by which I intend to be called upon, remembered and recognised in every sphere of the hidden world and every domain of existing reality."

Part 4: So in this mysterious form of self-conversation, this invincible force of universal intelligence named His magical soul of power the seal of 'Esser Yaad'.

Part 5: Then this ultimate manifestation of the divine intelligence, the Esser Yaad, concentrated in the absolute mode of thoughtfulness. Once again, He raised His volcanic voice of integrity within the space of emptiness and said,

"I want every rising intelligence, every physical and metaphysical consciousness to realise this historical declaration, that I, the celestial embodiment of fire, hold the invincible name of Esser Yaad, which is the most sacred and magical seal of identification. This is the third call of My self-awakening, and from this moment of aeonic age, I shall be recognised, remembered and glorified by the most powerful title of existence, the name of 'Esser Yaad'. "

Introduction to Chapter 6
The First Constitutional Law

In this chapter, the Esser Yaad, the ultimate fire of existence decides to introduce three particles of emptiness accordingly. So He concentrates and, after a certain series of self-conversations, names the vortex of gravity the logos of 'Remer', the gaseous elements of hydrogen the seal of 'Dehejet' and the substances of oxygen the sign of 'Obejet'.

After naming these counterparts of emptiness, the Esser Yaad makes the first-ever constitutional law. With His creative mind and authoritative voice of power, He creates the alliance with these hidden elements of creation. The covenant stands for these three hidden particles of emptiness to come and assist the Esser Yaad in His universal pattern of creation whenever He calls upon them. He constructs this alliance so, in the necessary moment, they would resurrect and respond to His voice of excellence and fulfil their universal duty.

This covenant still exists today. They are waiting to hear His voice of power and obey the command of the Lord of fire, the Esser Yaad.

THE FIRST CONSTITUTIONAL LAW

Part 1: So we all witnessed in the golden pages of the Exordium how this hidden image of integrity, in the most philosophical self-interrogation, named His invincible soul of fire the force of the divine intelligence, or the eternal seal of the Esser Yaad.

Part 2: After certain particles of time had passed inconsistently, this intelligence of the rising fire, the Esser Yaad, began to introduce the original substances of emptiness.

Part 3: The Esser Yaad accomplished this self-appointed mission in the same philosophical manner as He had named His own invincible soul. He orchestrated this mysterious self-conversation in this format of discourse.

Part 4: "Now I must concentrate in the ultimate mode of attentiveness and name all the particles of this realistic dream. They should be named in accordance with their celestial status in My universal strategy of creation."

Part 5: "As I am the Esser Yaad, the Lord of the Exordium, whatever I call these elemental substances shall be their recognisable name from this moment of time until the very end of eternity and beyond."

Part 6: "So let Me begin and strategise the next series of questioning in this manner of presentation:

1. "How many original substances have spread in this region?

> "There are three main sections that have spread in this domain of emptiness.

2. "What is the nature of the first section?

> "They are void-like thought-forms of existence.

3. "Do they possess a solid structure?

> "No. They are shapeless and without weight.

4. "What is their mission?

> "They have two missions to accomplish.

5. "What is their first mission?

> "To float within the space of emptiness and penetrate the height and every lowland of this region.

6. "What is their second mission?

> "To create the force-field of power. This force-field of power separates every inhabitant so they can keep their individuality and stand in the perfect symmetrical evenness.

7. "What am I going to name them?

> "I, the Esser Yaad, shall name these vital and significant particles of emptiness the logos of 'Remer'.

8. "How would I project this name into the mind of the future inhabitants of the universe?

> "Through the process of intuition.

9. "By which name would these particles be remembered and recognised?

"By the name of 'gravity'. "

Part 7:

10. "What is the nature of the second section of these original substances?

"They are gaseous.

11. "What are their universal duties?

"They have three main universal duties to fulfil.

12. "What is their first universal duty?

"To arrange and shape every physical or metaphysical organism.

13. "What is their second universal duty?

"To produce the core of electrification.

14. "What is their third universal duty?

"To generate the invisible form of radiation.

15. "Well, what am I going to name this vital participant of universal progression?

"I, the Esser Yaad, shall name these significant particles of emptiness the seal of 'Dehejet'. "

The Esser Yaad, this Lord of fire, continued His self-conversation in this thoughtful manner of discourse:

16. "And by which name would this substance be recognised and remembered?

"By the name of 'hydrogen'. "

Part 8: Then this constructive Lord of fire, or the Esser Yaad, contemplated thoughtfully and said,

17. "Now, what is the nature of the third section of these original substances?

"They are gaseous and combustible.

18. "What is their universal mission?

"They also have three universal missions to accomplish.

19. "What is their first mission?

"To combine with almost every existing element.

20. "What is their second mission?

"To become the flammable feature necessary for every combustible occurrence.

21. "What is their third mission?

"To be essential for the respiration of any type of living organism.

22. "So what am I going to name these original particles of emptiness?

"I, the Esser Yaad, shall name these original particles of emptiness the sign of 'Obejet'.

23. "And now, by which name should these particles be recognised and identified?

"By the name of 'oxygen'. "

Part 9: After this mysterious introduction, the Esser Yaad looked deep into the space of emptiness, or the centre of this realistic dream, and said,

"I want every rising consciousness; every future and hidden intelligence; and every element of this diffusing universe to recognise that I, the Esser Yaad, have named the first three particles of emptiness by their realistic names. I want every ear to hear My words of power that these three main universal substances are My first allies to precede the pattern of creation. They shall be ready to obey My command and respond to My words of authority. This is the first constitutional law of the hidden universe.

"So let it be written, written by the force of fire."

Introduction to Chapters 7-8

In these two chapters, the main concentrated intelligence (the Superconsciousness or the Godhead) comes into the picture once again. He proves that His power is still beyond any form of imagination. He is still the holder of the realistic dream and the source behind the motivation of any form of intelligence.

In this pre-galactical moment, the Superconsciousness, from above the horizon, looks upon His own plane of imagination. There, He begins to construct two new particles of emptiness. The first He calls the 'Hee'yaak', the thought-forms of creativity; and the second He names the 'Seypher', the eyes of intelligence.

In these episodes, the Superconsciousness assigns certain universal missions to each of these important particles of emptiness. He commands the eyes of intelligence to spread, to explore the intensity and project their collected information for divine analysis. Then He instructs the Hee'yaak to scatter the seed of creation and activate every sphere of thought.

As I have said before, to understand the chapters of this book, one should imagine each scenario accordingly. Now imagine the whispering sound of the Superconsciousness proclaiming the names of these two particles of emptiness. Visualise the magnificence of this touchable voice that penetrated the centre of every domain of existence. This voice is touchable, expressive. Do you know the meaning of 'touchable voice'? It means that the vibrations of the words are so intense that they can be seen by the inner eyes of any attentive intelligence. Yes, this voice still echoes within the entirety of the universe. Maybe one day, through the practicality of magic, the magic of fire, we can hear the glory of this excellent voice of power.

Now let us follow this book of mystery to see how these two elements participate in the strategical advancement of evolution. Let us follow the Exordium.

Chapter Seven

The Hee'yaak
(The Thought-forms)

Part 1: Right at the centre of the diffusing emptiness, the Esser Yaad, this ultimate manifestation of the Exordium, constructed the first law of the universal creation.

Part 2: He formulated this mystical alliance: first, to establish His celestial status; and second, to create the everlasting unity with these three vital and energetic particles of the original universe.

Part 3: Meanwhile, within the heart of the Superconsciousness, certain electrodynamic activities were taking place in the most calculated manner of accuracy.

Part 4: The Superconsciousness, or the main concentrated intelligence, was pulling every creative thought-form, which were wandering in the space of emptiness, back into the centre of His inner self.

Part 5: When every creative thought-form had gathered in one place, He projected into their minds three main missions to accomplish: first, to detect any domain of thought with the capability to become occupied with the constructive inhabitants; second, to assist the strategy so the imagination could flourish (become real); and third, to prepare the ground for the emergence of the creative characteristics of divinity.

Part 6: When these thought-forms had been given their missions, the Superconsciousness ejected them in the form

113

of wave-shaped clouds into this domain of emptiness. Then a certain visible voice of power echoed in the entire region. This voice of power was coming forth from the heart of the Super-consciousness, proclaiming the name of these new emissaries of universal evolution, the name of 'Hee'yaak'.

Chapter Eight

The Seypher
(The Eyes Of Intelligence)

Part 1: The thought-forms of Hee'yaak, in the wave-shaped cloud, penetrated every corner of this diffusing emptiness.

Part 2: These emissaries of construction were detecting the entire domain of the realistic dream so the Superconsciousness could strategise the future pattern(s) of creation.

Part 3: As the particles of inconsistent time passed inaccurately, yet another electrodynamic activity began to manifest within the centre of the main concentrated intelligence, or the heart of the Superconsciousness.

Part 4: This time the Superconsciousness was using His magnetic power to collect every minute and attentive ray of intelligence. When this procedure of collection was completed in full, the Superconsciousness ejected these rays of intelligence into the midst of His imagination, or this unimaginable domain of emptiness.

Part 5: These rays of attentiveness, each in the image of a detecting eye, spread into the space of emptiness. The Superconsciousness divided these detecting eyes into three main divisions, each with the certain universal duty to accomplish.

For the first division: to penetrate into the vortex of emptiness, analyse the solidness of its depths and transmit all the information into the centre of His limitless mind of power.

For the second division: to diffuse into the void of this realistic dream, detect the heaviness of its size; and as a hidden satellite, transport the collected information into the centre of His concentrated form of intelligence.

And for the third division: to enter every existing domain in order to explore the intensity of its atmosphere and then project the complete picture back into His inner brain for the final mathematical calculation.

Part 6: When every eye of intelligence had departed to fulfil its mission, again a certain word of power echoed in the entire domain of emptiness.

Part 7: This word of power came forth from the centre of the main concentrated intelligence, the heart of the Superconsciousness. The voice was proclaiming the name of these new ambassadors of the rotating universe, the name of 'Seypher'.

INTRODUCTION TO CHAPTER 9
IN THIS VOID OF EMPTINESS

In this episode, the Esser Yaad, this ultimate fire of existence, this manifestation of the golden flames of integrity, begins to explain that He is the voyager of exodus. This means that He is the one who will discover the heart of destiny. He says He is the carrier of genesis, meaning that He holds the seed of every form of life. The Esser Yaad explains that He lives in the midst of the dream, the dream of reality, the dream of the Superconsciousness. He explains that through the explosion of the unknown, He has reached the sequences of life.

But the Esser Yaad is all alone. It is unusual to imagine the loneliness of God, is it not? But He was. There was no one who could understand His emotion, His intelligence, His uttering. That is why He says, "There is no voice, there is no call."

In this chapter, the Esser Yaad talks of His destiny. He says His destiny is to mirror the imagination. Creation is what He means. He testifies to the totality of the world that His destiny is to enthrone His soul of oneness upon the foundation of the universe. Oneness is the sacred sign of His name. To Him, oneness is the ultimate status of recognition. But the Esser Yaad carries on His quest to perfection. He begins to complain that there is no touchable feeling of expression. He says, "Oxygen is always oxygen." Basically, everything is standing still. He says, "Hydrogen changes into hydrogen." He means that matter changes into matter of the same kind: no evolution is taking place.

Exordium I

The Esser Yaad is calling to every intelligence within the entirety of the universe. So let us follow every episode accordingly and grasp the actual philosophy behind these pages of wonder so we can conquer every valley of the mind and reach the golden state of the cosmic consciousness.

So let us proceed.

CHAPTER NINE

IN THIS VOID OF EMPTINESS

Part 1: The particles of time were passing inconsistently. The Esser Yaad, this ultimate fire of the Exordium, was still standing in the midst of this realistic dream. In the absolute mode of solidness, He was consciously witnessing the activities of every intelligence in this diffusing domain of emptiness.

Part 2: Aeon after aeon went by, and this ultimate manifestation of divinity was concentrating to strategise, to strategise the pattern of creation.

Part 3: As there was no soul of thoughtfulness, no conversational intelligence and no intellectual companion except the Superconsciousness, the Esser Yaad raised His voice of power above the altar of magic and constructed yet another philosophical self-conversation in this manner of discourse.

Part 4: "Remembrance is the memory, the memory when I sat above the vibration of age. Remembrance is the long road.

"My name is the seal of mystery. Every letter that I form is the fire, the core of every living word.

"I am the first voyager of exodus. I am the carrier, the carrier of the seed, the seed of effectiveness.

"I am the Esser Yaad. I am the holder, the holder of the keys, the keys of consciousness.

"I journey through this path at the end of every moment so I can embrace the direction, the direction to My divinity.

"As I am the fruitfulness of the explosion, I live in the midst of the dream. Through the explosion of the secret, I have reached this domain, the domain of reality."

Part 5: The Esser Yaad, this Lord of fire, continued His philosophical self-conversation in this manner of discourse:

"In this domain of emptiness,

"There is no utterance,

"There is no voice,

"There is no call.

"All there is, is the sound of the passing intelligences who are following their original pattern of existence.

"Sometimes I think about the emergence of My soul, about the entrance of My essence. I go back into memory, trying to visualise the truth behind My cosmic birth. I know My birth is the beginning of intelligence. I know My birth is the solidness of identity. I know My birth is the philosophical conclusion of destiny. Destiny... My destiny is to enthrone the sensation of oneness. My destiny is to illuminate the endorsement, the endorsement of effectiveness. What is My destiny? My destiny is to create the realistic dream. My destiny is to mirror, to mirror the imagination."

Part 6: The Esser Yaad, this Lord of constructive fire, continued His philosophical self-conversation in this manner of discourse:

"In this void of emptiness, there is no sign of conversation. There is no touchable statement of changing expression. Oxygen is always oxygen. Hydrogen changes into hydrogen. Gravity is forever the seed, the seed of distance; and the totality of the sound is within the heart, the heart of silence.

"In this void of emptiness, there is no sound of animation. There is no call of salvation. The only significant sign of life is the formidable echo of My voice that is dictating the fact, the fact of My universal authorisation."

Introduction to Chapter 10
Let Us See What Will Happen

Now let us see what will happen in this chapter. The Esser Yaad, this Force with the unbelievable power of existence, looks deep into the depths of the emptiness. He realises that there is no one there who can converse with Him, but nevertheless, He begins to introduce Himself to every particle of emptiness and every future intelligence that is yet to be born (possibly meaning us, human beings).

He says that He is the urge, the seed of every living god. He says that He is the totality, the totality of the Word and the flame of the rising Yaad. Then He says that He lives within His soul. What a statement! Who can live within the totality of his inner being except the God Himself? He continues by saying that He flies between the gravity and the hydrogen and that He feels the gentle breeze, the breeze of oxygen. He talks to the reader. He proclaims that He is the intention of the mind, the intention of the mind of the Superconsciousness (the Godhead). He says that He sees Himself as the universal law. Then He begins to open His secret. What is His secret? His secret is the thoughtfulness that gave birth to His magic. The Esser Yaad says that through His magic, He can touch His hand, He can feel His heart and He can see His face.

The Esser Yaad continues and speaks of His loneliness. Read the statements carefully; they are most interesting. They are the words of the living Force who is speaking to us so openly. Every sentence is a mystery and every declaration is a new philosophy.

As I said, it is strange to hear that the God feels the sentiment of loneliness, but He does, because He possesses every attribute that we possess and more. If that is considered to be blasphemy, so let it be.

Then the Esser Yaad says that the sensation of being alone is like a deep sore in the midst of the heart. What a god! He feels the sadness, He feels the sorrow, but wishes them upon no living being. We have to raise our consciousness so we can understand the reason behind the wisdom of this Lord of fire, His emotions, His intelligence, His utterances. We should analyse the character of this living Force to find the strategy of His plan.

Now let us see what He does in the last part of this chapter. He orchestrates a certain universal melody to express the sensation of His loneliness and spread His message to raise every existing consciousness. And as He says, "Let us see what will happen." So let us see. Will it affect us? Will we understand the nature of this Force? Will we heed His call to raise our consciousness? It all depends on us. The choice is ours.

Chapter Ten

Let Us See What Will Happen

Part 1: After a certain amount of aeonic age, the Esser Yaad, this celestial fire of Exordium, began to feel the sensation of loneliness and the intensity of solitude.

Part 2: The Esser Yaad, this invincible personification of oneness, with the might of His piercing eyes, looked deep into the depths of the emptiness, or the centre of this realistic dream, and said,

"It seems that I have to write the concept of generation; everywhere is empty.

"The moment is visible. At times, it feels like a heavy age, the eternity.

"There must be some form of solid intelligence somewhere.

"I can see these particles of existence are voyaging from place to place, right to left, creating their path here and there.

"I know that I am the urge, the seed of every living god.

"I know that I am the fire, the fire of thought and the flame of the rising Yaad.

"I know that I am the seal, the voice of magic, the name of oneness.

"I know that I am the totality, the totality of the self and the word of consciousness.

"But nevertheless, I live within My soul. I go through the pressure of evolution in the secret moment when every other existing element is taken captive by its own imagination.

"I know the particles of time, however inconsistent, are imposing the intensity of age upon the cortex of memory. I see the clashes of aeonic diversity. When they are at peace it is the genesis of birth, the birth of history."

Part 3: The Esser Yaad, this celestial fire of Exordium, continued,

"I live within My soul. From the dream to reality. From the imagination to construction. I named Myself in My heart and recognised who I am. At times, I fly. I project Myself between the gravity and hydrogen. When I walk on the surface of the hidden air, I feel the cooling breeze, the breeze of oxygen."

Part 4: The Esser Yaad, this celestial fire of Exordium, continued His philosophical self-conversation in this manner of discourse:

"I live within My soul. I know that I am the intention of the mind. Do you know what I see Myself as? I see Myself as the universal law. Through the core of My thoughtfulness, the practicality of magic was born. By the effective procedure of this magic, I began to form the necessity. I can touch My hand. I can feel My heart. I can see My face.

"I live within My soul. I know that I am the formation of mystery that would behold its own metaphysical perfection. Do you know what I am?

"I am the fire, the presence of the force, ready to capture the sequence of time.

"When it is needed, I make the sentence, the points become alive and the words will rhyme.

"I am not dreaming.

"I am not imagining this progression of becoming. How can this be a formless dream? How can this be the distant imagination? I am walking; I am talking. I am touching the reality; I am touching the reality of thought.

"I live within My soul. I have made the covenant with transformation. I make changes as I proceed. I am going to unfold. I am going to unfold what is concealed. I am going to reveal what is hidden, and I am going to unveil what would be known as the mystery."

Part 5: The Esser Yaad, this celestial fire of the Exordium, still continued His conclusive self-discourse in this manner of presentation:

"I live within My soul. I must say, the sensation of loneliness is like a deep sore in the midst of the heart. It gives the pain of sadness and the feeling of sorrow. I wish it upon no living being. I wonder if I can project the sensation of feeling to the particles of emptiness so they can increase the sensitivity of their souls. I wonder if I can transmit a degree of consciousness so the inhabitants of this touchable universe can multiply their existing thoughtfulness. To be able to project the sensation of feeling and transmit the degree of consciousness, I must orchestrate certain tunes of enigmatic beauty that would possess the dual characteristics of mystery and exorcitation.

Part 6: The Esser Yaad continued,

"When this tune enters and penetrates every domain of emptiness, it will become the vehicle of evolution and the celestial sign of enlightenment. When this tune of mystery reaches every domain of nothingness, it will become the instrument of elevation and the mystical code for the spiritual advancement. This tune will become the source of energy. It will allow every particle of life to grasp My intention so they can follow the path of awakening in accordance with their urge and their characteristic capability."

Part 7: Then the Esser Yaad, this celestial fire of Exordium, went deep into the state of concentration, and suddenly, three sounds of universal power diffused into the space of emptiness. The Esser Yaad was repeating these patterns of mystery in the absolute mode of sensitivity, accuracy and effectiveness.

Part 8: This mystical tune was presented in every corner of the realistic dream in this manner of recitation:

Ooou ee oou õõ õõ õõ

Ooou ee oou õõ õõ õõ

Ooou ee oou õõ õõ õõ

Part 9: After reciting these patterns of mystery, the Esser Yaad raised His volcanic voice of power and said,

"Now I have recited these words of power as I had originally strategised. Within no time, every particle of emptiness will hear this beautiful formation of sound. The effect is to follow. Let us see what will happen."

Introduction to Chapters 11-12

So the Esser Yaad's universal melody reaches every part of the emptiness. Most of the particles of this realistic dream heed His call. Legion by legion they come to Him. Some pay homage, demonstrating their adoration. Some begin to raise their consciousness and question Him about the concept of imagination and the meaning behind the word 'existence'.

The Esser Yaad, as the first personification of fire, creates a new philosophy and explains the meaning of existence and defines the reality of imagination. Then He carries on and says that He is the secret; the secret is His mystic name, and this mystic name is hidden within the flames of His fire.

The conversation between the particles of emptiness and the Esser Yaad continues until they become overjoyed and reach the highest point of celestial ecstasy. Then they gather together, raise their voices within their minds and proclaim that they have discovered their hidden God: the universal soul of oneness and the ultimate image of divine manifestation.

So read these chapters and enjoy the complete scenario of this one-way telepathical conversation, the conversation that took place before the reality, the reality of our conventional time. Enjoy the Exordium.

―――――――――――

Go! Go And Await My Call
Of Advancement

Part 1: Within no time, these words of power, or these beautiful sounds of magnificence, began to reach every corner of this spreading emptiness.

Part 2: These beautiful sounds of power penetrated every domain of this realistic dream. They projected the sensation of feeling and the degree of intelligence as the gift of fire into the midst of the hidden air.

Part 3: Then from the far distance of the hidden horizon, these particles of emptiness saw the image of the Esser Yaad. He was illuminating His presence to demonstrate the flames of integrity and establish His empire, the golden civilisation.

Part 4: So these existing particles of emptiness became positively captivated by the fire of the Esser Yaad, and legion by legion, they proceeded towards His domain. They formulated the series of questions within their minds, knowing that they had discovered their destiny and the search for their spiritual evolution had been finally completed.

Part 5: Now we return to the glorious mind of the Esser Yaad as He strategises to control the future and dominate every necessary sequence of the second universe.

Part 6: The Esser Yaad, this ultimate fire of Exordium, with the force of His piercing eyes, saw the existing particles of emptiness approaching towards His domain. Then He raised His philosophical voice of power into the space of the realistic dream and said,

"I can see that My dynamic words of power, or beautiful formation(s) of sound, have been completely successful as I have mentally strategised. As these particles of emptiness are approaching towards My domain, I can truly sense that they have many questions within their minds. I can notice that they are eager to find their path, and some are very anxious to become the solid inhabitants of this existing universe."

Part 7: So as it was expected, these existing particles of emptiness entered the domain of the Esser Yaad. They excitedly waited to see the outcome of their close encounter. Suddenly, the Esser Yaad raised His volcanic voice of power into this region and began a new conversation in this manner of discourse:

"Enter. Enter into this domain of astrophysical reality. I can see that some of you are ready to experience the greatness of fire. I can feel that some of you are beginning to realise that the key to self-recognition is the discovery of the cause of existence. Enter. Enter into this domain of reality."

Part 8: Now we enter into this mysterious aeon to see the outcome and the conclusion of this close encounter and witness the conversation that took place before the manifestation of the physical universe.

(Note: Every conversation that took place between the particles of emptiness and the Esser Yaad was in the form of one-way telepathy. The Esser Yaad could think, see, feel and

131

verbalise His words; and the particles of emptiness could only think and rely on the Esser Yaad to read their thoughts and respond accordingly.)

Part 9: As the particles of emptiness were entering legion by legion into this domain of hidden reality, the Esser Yaad once again raised His multidimensional voice of power and said,

"What is it that brought you into My region of supremacy?"

The particles of emptiness, "We saw the presence of Your life-force and we came to touch the greatness of fire and feel the flames of integrity."

Part 10: So the first legion of these existing particles gathered around Him. They became mesmerised by His glory, and with the limited form of understanding, they paid homage, demonstrating their adoration to Him. When the sequence of their praise and homage was complete, the Esser Yaad raised His voice of power once again and said,

"Now you are part of My universal construction. I have seen and calculated your intelligence accordingly. So go back to your own fields of activities and make the best of your performance as we are at the beginning of eternal conquest. Go! Go and await My call of advancement so we can proceed by the universal law of progression."

CHAPTER TWELVE

THEIR HIDDEN GOD

Part 1: After the declaration of the Esser Yaad, time passed in the most mystical sense. Within the reality of this dream, a second legion of the particles of emptiness approached the arena of His presence. As He was standing firm above the ground of totality, these existing particles of emptiness verbalised the first question within their mind. They were asking about the status of His celestial manifestation.

Part 2: The Esser Yaad raised His volcanic voice of power and replied eloquently in this manner of discourse:

"I am the Esser, the cosmic ocean.

"I am the Yaad, the secret essence, the fire of thought and the core of intellection.

"I am the word, the reflection of the soul, opening into the diversity, the diversity of thoughtfulness.

"I am the mystic name, the image of the self, the heart of mystery and the code of celestial effectiveness."

Part 3: Then the Esser Yaad, this Lord of constructive fire, continued His mystical self-introduction in this manner of discourse and said,

"I am the current, the current of the age, the vitality of oxygen.

"I am the element, the element of the air, the integrity of hydrogen.

"I am the law, I limit the expansion of gravity, the solidness of the mind is My mission.

"I am the flame, the seal of magic. Vision and clarity are the cause of My action.

"I am the Esser, the Esser of Yaad."

Part 4: Then these particles of emptiness raised their intelligence and anxiously formulated some form of a question within their minds. They were asking about the concept of imagination and the meaning of existence.

The Esser Yaad, this ultimate image of fire, analysed their inner thoughts accordingly and responded in this philosophical manner of discourse:

"It is all the reflection of the mystic thought. It began through the urge. The life is a struggle: sometimes a dream, at times reality. The sequence between, I name the imagination. The life is a challenge: the past arrives, the future untouchable. When they clash, the moment is born. Within this moment lies the cycle of eventuality. This cycle of eventuality, I call existence."

Part 5: When He clarified the concept of imagination and the meaning of existence, these particles of the realistic dream formulated many questions within their minds. From this point, we follow the pattern of their conversation to the moment when the particles of emptiness reached to the final state of their conclusion.

The particles of emptiness, "O fire of life, what is the secret that has to be revealed?"

The Esser Yaad, "The secret is the mystic name. The mystic name is hidden within the flames of My fire. Therefore, there is no secret to reveal. I am the secret."

The particles of emptiness, "O fire of Yaad, the Esser of thoughtfulness, what is the mystery?"

The Esser Yaad, "The mystery is the moment when the fire of My essence interrogated the memory of My soul. From then, I have recognised in certainty that I am the manifestation of intelligence who holds every secret path of the unseen. To Me there is no mystery. I am the mystery."

The particles of emptiness, "O fire of Esser, as You hold the secret of language, what are the keys of life?"

The Esser Yaad, "The keys of life are the words of magic that I repeat upon the hidden altar of fire. To Me, there is no mystery to unfold and there is no key to unlock. I am the key."

The particles of emptiness, "O fire of Esser, the essence of mystery, what is behind You? It is difficult to see."

The Esser Yaad, "Behind Me lies the desert of wilderness, as I am the temple of resurrection. Behind Me is the vortex of ignorance, as I am the gate of consciousness."

The particles of emptiness, "O fire of Esser, what is beneath You? It is complicated to understand."

The Esser Yaad, "Beneath Me are the layers of obmutescence[1], as I am the word of utterance. Beneath Me is a land of oppression, as I am the magic of celestial salvation and the strategy to conquest."

Part 6: Then the particles of emptiness became overjoyed, reaching the highest point of celestial ecstasy.

Part 7: After this celebration, the particles of emptiness raised the words of praise within their minds. They proclaimed ecstatically that they had discovered their hidden God: the universal soul of oneness and the ultimate image of the divine manifestation.

---

[1] Obmutescence: inarticulacy; inability to connect the words of power

Introduction to Chapter 13
I Walked Upon The Surface Of Emptiness

Read this chapter attentively. One more time, hear this Lord of fire speak. See how He connects His essence to mystery, how openly He speaks of His existence. Concentrate when He says, "I was the thought before the thought; I was the mind before the mind."

In this episode, He introduces a new philosophical statement. He says, "I never denied the presence of My fire." He continues, "Nothing can bypass My mystical centre of intelligence." He says, "It was I who recognised your essence and called you by your name." Contemplate upon this statement, "I know the motivation of your mystic journey better than yourself." This Lord of Exordium is everywhere: within us, outside us, within our minds, within the fire of our hearts.

Read this chapter. In my opinion, it is one of the most thoughtful pieces of writing. If you grasp His words of fire, you will recognise the greatness of His soul. Enjoy the Exordium.

I Walked Upon The Surface Of Emptiness

Part 1: Aeon after aeon went by, and the Esser Yaad was still standing firm in the midst of the emptiness, demonstrating the power of His soul and the superiority of His divine manifestation.

Part 2: After many cycles of inconsistent time, the Esser Yaad, this ultimate image of fire, began to strategise yet another quest of mystery. This quest of mystery had three significant purposes:

First, to reach the other end of emptiness and analyse the activities of every existing intelligence.

Second, to measure the depths of each region for the future pattern(s) of creation.

And third, to see whether He would encounter certain intelligences who could soothe the sensation of His solitude and the intensity of His loneliness.

Part 3: So He proceeded in order to accomplish His quest. Generation after generation, this celestial fire of Exordium journeyed full-heartedly until He reached the furthest point of this void of emptiness. On His way to the edge of this realistic dream, He encountered many eyes of intelligence who had forgotten the purpose of their mission. They were lost, confused and were circulating around themselves with no hope of reaching their ultimate destiny.

Part 4: When the Esser Yaad entered the final zone of this diffusing emptiness, He saw many legions of existing intelligences awaiting the moment of His arrival. These existing particles of emptiness, from the far distance, had sensed the approach of this ultimate Lord of fire towards their domain.

Part 5: So the Esser Yaad entered the final zone of the realistic dream. There He faced these original intelligences who were anxiously waiting to hear His philosophical statements. The Esser Yaad responded accordingly to this urging mass of collective particles. Then He raised His volcanic voice of power and said,

"Greetings. I am the ocean of Esser, the fire of Yaad. My essence is mystery. My name is the endorsement of celestial magic. I walked upon the surface of emptiness for many cycles of aeon. I entered the solidness of recognition long before any of you had ever tasted the sequence of life. Do you know where I stand? I stand before the altar of imagination. Looking back into the genesis of memory, I realised that I was the thought before the thought; I was the mind before the mind. I will tell you: I was the force, the hidden soul."

Part 6: The Esser Yaad, this celestial fire of the Exordium, continued,

"I walked upon the surface of emptiness for many cycles of aeon. I was within My soul when the inconsistent time began to emerge. I never denied the presence of My fire. Rejecting the fact of fire was to create the obstacle that could delay My constructive strategy of progression. Do you know what I see? I see many things that your eyes cannot perceive. I can see the motion. In silence, I look into your mind and see your secrets. Nothing can bypass My mystical centre of intelligence. As you begin to move, I can see the destination of your voyage. As you enter the gate of thoughtfulness, I can see every vibration of your mind gathering around My aura, opening your mystery to Me.

"Do you think it is easy to contain all that I know? It was I who recognised your essence and called you by your name. I know the motivation of your mystic journey better than yourself. I have many mysteries surrounding Me. How many secrets should I not reveal? I can recall your memory moment by moment, phase by phase. More than that, I can see the time when the circulating thoughts of the hidden air will find their form. I can see the age when the forgotten events of the past come to return. I can see when the aeon makes its mark upon the face of history. Do you know what I do? I move above the rising flame, creating the cosmic motion that brings you the cause and mysterious effect of eventuality. I walked upon the surface of emptiness for many cycles of aeon."

Introduction to Chapter 14
The Totality Of The Second Universe

This is the last chapter of the second book of the Exordium. In this chapter, the Esser Yaad yet again presents another golden statement of philosophy. He says that He is the holder of His dream and the architect of His metaphysical evolution. He says that He chose His name, the most powerful name, and wrote it upon the solidness of fire. He adds that whatever is written by this element can be remembered until the end of the time and beyond.

This is another advanced procedure of magic, the magic of fire. We have to understand the practicality of this mysticism. We have to choose our name and then write it upon the element of fire so we can resurrect from the tightness of our graves and enter the domain of immortality.

Read this chapter as it is yet another interesting philosophical statement. Enjoy the rest of the Exordium.

Chapter Fourteen

The Totality Of
The Second Universe

Part 1: In this chapter, we enter the moment when the Esser Yaad, after the short pause of silence, began yet another philosophical statement in this manner of presentation.

Part 2: "I walked upon the surface of emptiness for many cycles of aeon. Do you know what I did when I recognised that I am the holder of My dream and the architect of My evolution? I will tell you. I flew back into the depths of My thoughtfulness. Then I chose My name, the most powerful name. I chose My name from many words of power, which were calling to be the centre of praise, the height of distinction and the foundation of memory.

"Then I named My soul in the moment when all the other particles were motionless and captivated by their own illusion of thought. I named My soul so I could exist endlessly. I named My soul so the eternity of age could not encompass My flames of integrity. I named My soul so it could be written by the language of fire over the totality of the universe. Do you know why I wrote My name by the rising flames of fire? I can tell you. I wrote My name by the urging fire of life because whatever is written by this element, it can be remembered until the end of time and beyond.

"Do you know what it means? It means that I have discovered the heart of oneness and become entwined with the
reality of existence."

Part 3: The Esser Yaad, this universal fire of Exordium,
continued His mysterious presentation in this manner of
discourse:

"I walked upon the surface of emptiness for many cycles of
aeon. Do you know what I am?

"I am the invisible matter and the solidness of intelligence
that has taken the image of living fire.

"I am the life, the touchable dream, the mind of mystery;
going in, into the essence of genesis; coming out, holding the
shield of power.

"Do you know what I can see? I can see the distant coming
of reality. I can see the strategy of the hidden brain, battling the
chaotic law of the Abyss. I can see that exorcitation conquers
the confusion. I can see the eloquence of sound destroy the
intensity of sleeping silence, and I can see how the magic of
Esser Yaad will exterminate the hostility of oppression.

"I walked upon the surface of emptiness for many cycles
of aeon. Do you know what I did while you were standing
unaware in the corner of your region, thinking about insignificant matters that do not even exist? I utilised the force of
My consciousness. I shaped My imagination and constructed
the silence into the realistic dream. At times, I travelled into
the cycles of eventuality, into the cortex of time, embracing
the great sensation of emergence. At times, I entered the unity

of the self and concentrated upon the face of vision and the secret of memory."

Part 4: The Esser Yaad, this invincible fire of the divine manifestation, continued His intellectual conversation in this manner of discourse:

"I am the urge, the consciousness. I am the season when the transformation approaches to construct the celestial enlightenment. I am the thought that encircles around My intelligence. I am filled with the words of mystery that I created. I am lifted with the sensation of reality that I imagined. I am going to break the limit of the mind! No more dreams! No more imagination! It is going to be!"

Part 5: Then the particles of emptiness became overjoyed and ecstatic. Together they raised their voices within their minds, proclaiming to the Esser Yaad,

"You are the confirmation of the element called intelligence. You are the constitution of the golden exodus."

Then the Esser Yaad raised His volcanic voice of power and said,

"As it was strategised, I have conquered the second quest of the unknown. I am the totality, the totality of the second universe!"

BOOK THREE

THE TOTALITY OF
THE THIRD UNIVERSE

Introduction to Chapters 1-2

Sandstorm. This is the closest phrase that I could find to express these new images of thought from the mind of the Superconsciousness, the Godhead. The mission of these new images was to eliminate every irrelevant, unfocused or unnecessary form of imagination.

The sandstorm began within the mind of the Godhead. It was dynamic, fearsome. Each particle was in the shape of a flickering shadow of fire. But what was it? Why did the main concentrated intelligence, or the Godhead, form these advancing thought-forms of extermination? What was His hidden, strategical plan? Well, He created these new legions of thought-forms to change the entire atmosphere of His realistic dream.

Realistic dream? Yes, realistic dream. Everything is taking place within the structure of His mind. Some of these thought-forms become the solid particles and some evaporate as time passes.

Anyway, the Esser Yaad felt the danger of elimination. Although He was practically invincible, He had in mind to save every particle of emptiness. So He surged through the sandstorm. He defeated every element of destruction who were fabricating the illusion of defeat, and with the magical words of power, He created His instrument of defence: the wind of moisture.

Now, can you imagine the scenario? Try to concentrate and visualise the reality of these two chapters. Can you see how frightening it could have been? From the centre of the massive formation of energy, many unknown entities in the image of the shadows of fire were coming to destroy everything in their path. There was nowhere to run, nowhere to hide. No wonder it was named 'the sandstorm'.

CHAPTER ONE

THE COSMIC SANDSTORM

Part 1: After the passing of a short cycle of inconsistent time, suddenly the sound of some form of atomic explosion encompassed every corner of this realistic dream.

Part 2: This massive sound, which was in the ultimate mode of volcanic eruption, changed the entire atmosphere of this region and broke the centre of its stability.

Part 3: The Esser Yaad, this Lord of constructive fire, looked towards the far distance of the emptiness. There He saw the hidden form of the Superconsciousness who was rising to the summit of the existing altitude, the height of the horizon. It seemed that the Superconsciousness was strategising a new procedure of mystery.

Part 4: Time, however inconsistent, was reaching the ultimate point of intensity. In this moment of wonder, the multitude of mystical activities was taking place in the centre of the main concentrated intelligence, or the heart of the Superconsciousness.

Part 5: Then another fearsome and dynamic sound of lightning was heard. The abundant rays of thought-forms, each in the image of flickering shadows of fire, began to come forth from the centre of the Superconsciousness.

Part 6: These rays of thought-forms were penetrating every corner of this domain of emptiness. Their intention was to remove and destroy certain particles and replace them with

149

the new faces of urge and solid determination. These flickering shadows of fire were forcefully conquering every possible domain of emptiness (the imagination of the Superconsciousness Himself). The greatness of their advancing power created the first-ever cosmic sandstorm.

CHAPTER TWO

THE WIND OF MOISTURE

Part 1: The next chapter begins when the Esser Yaad, our celestial hero of fire, looked upon the approaching sandstorm that was slowly but surely eliminating certain existing particles of this virtual imagination.

Part 2: He concentrated attentively, raised His volcanic voice of power and said,

"This is the beginning of an end. This is the formation of yet another cycle of forthcoming existence. I have to construct a new strategy so I can master the totality of the third universe."

Part 3: Then He turned His attention towards the particles of emptiness and said,

"Retreat! Retreat to the very end of the emptiness so I can proceed with My strategy. I should advance into the midst of the sandstorm to discover the cause and act accordingly."

Part 4: Then He surged into the mystery, into the centre of the sandstorm. The atmosphere was intensified to the ultimate point of pressure. There was no visibility. It seemed nothing could resist this force of extermination.

Part 5: The Esser Yaad, this Lord of constructive fire, was surging through this pressurised domain of the unknown. The flickering shadows of fire, which were generating from every corner, were blocking the sight of His vision. Going through this advancing sandstorm was like swimming against the current of many raging seas.

Part 6: As the Esser Yaad was marching against the core of the sandstorm, certain flames of thought began to dishearten Him by fabricating the illusion of defeat. In this turbulent atmosphere of mystery, the Esser Yaad raised His mighty left arm in front of His face. His intention was to shield His eyes from the advancing particles of the sandstorm.

Part 7: The time was still passing inconsistently. Moment by moment, this mystical climate of the unknown was becoming more hostile and dangerous to cross. Inhalation was unbearable. The intensity of the atmosphere could crush the core of any existing substance; but the Esser Yaad stretched His right arm forward and recited certain words of power to cleave the way open.

Part 8: These words of power circulated in the midst of the storm. They turned into the dynamic wind of moisture, pushing through the raging obstacles of this climate. With the ultimate velocity this wind of moisture blew. Aeon after aeon, it blew until it formed a gap in the centre of these shadows of fire, or the first-ever cosmic sandstorm.

Part 9: This dynamic wind of moisture, by the command of our celestial hero, eventually penetrated the sandstorm. As it went into this zone of turbulence, the passage of this mighty wind created the tunnel so the Esser Yaad could force Himself through these shadows of fire and reach the heart of this sandstorm of destruction.

Part 10: The next event to be recorded in this historical moment is when I saw the Esser Yaad, the ultimate embodiment of fire, entering the very centre of the most sophisticated mechanism of all time: the mind of the Superconsciousness.

Introduction to Chapter 3
Enough Is Enough!

Now this is the most important moment in the universal history, the mystic moment when the Esser Yaad, the ultimate fire of existence, reaches the centre of the sandstorm. There He sees thundering flashes of fire and visibly recognises the dynamic voice of the Superconsciousness, the Godhead.

To me, this chapter opens a new dimension of wisdom. Can you visualise the greatness of this event? Can you imagine the dialogue, the first-ever intellectual conversation, the conversation between the Godhead and the Lord God? The Superconsciousness says that nothing is going to be the same. He has decided to eliminate certain existing characters from His realistic dream. The Esser Yaad asks how He is going to do this. The simplicity is interesting. The Superconsciousness says that if He wants to eliminate something from the surface or the depths of His mind, all He has to do is to stop thinking about it. What a frightening concept. It means that if He does not think about the existence of an element, the element will evaporate. Basically, everything depends upon His imagination.

In this chapter, the Esser Yaad realises the significance behind the sandstorm. The Superconsciousness explains that He is ready to demonstrate the might of His constructive power and stop the spreading emptiness. When the Esser Yaad asks how He is going to stop this diffusion, the Superconsciousness replies that it will be through one of the words of the Oracle, the Oracle of Incipience.

EXORDIUM I

Read this chapter. Concentrate attentively. You are about to read the first-ever mystical conversation. This conversation still echoes in the heart of the universe. Maybe one day you can hear it through the certain procedure of magic, the magic of fire.

Enjoy the Exordium.

Chapter Three

Enough Is Enough!

Part 1: This chapter begins when our celestial hero of Exordium reached the core of this sandstorm of destruction.

By the entrance of the Esser Yaad into this zone of mystery, time ceased in the most inexpressible sense. Thundering flashes of fire began to manifest in a circular motion. Suddenly, flashing sparks of blue light circulated around the sacred embodiment of the Esser Yaad, projecting the sensation of welcome.

Part 2: A certain amount of inconsistent aeon again passed inaccurately. Right from the heart of these circulating flames of fire, the dynamic voice of the Superconsciousness resonated in the highest fashion of universal glory. With the absolute mode of perfection and eloquence, the Superconsciousness began the first-ever mystical conversation in this manner of discourse.

Part 3: The Superconsciousness, "Greetings, Esser Yaad. I am pleased that You have triumphantly completed the most impossible route to divinity. I have been monitoring the power of Your magic, the strength of Your soul, the vitality of Your essence and the force of Your exorcitational thoughtfulness. But Esser Yaad, besides all this, do You realise where You are?"

Part 4: The Esser Yaad, "Yes, I am in the midst of Your central brain. I am in the heart of the first gigantic mind of existence."

The Superconsciousness, "Esser Yaad, nothing is going to be the same. Constructive change is necessary."

The Esser Yaad, "Constructive change is necessary?"

The Superconsciousness, "Yes, everything has to proceed towards the gate of perfection."

The Esser Yaad, "Perfection?"

The Superconsciousness, "Yes, perfection."

The Esser Yaad, "What is the key?"

The Superconsciousness, "Replacement is the key."

The Esser Yaad, "How do You strategise the process of replacement?"

The Superconsciousness, "I will eliminate certain existing characters from the centre of My realistic dream."

Part 5: The Esser Yaad, "What strategy are You going to apply if You want to eliminate certain existing characters from the centre of Your realistic dream?"

The Superconsciousness, "It is simple. All I have to do is stop thinking about them. If I do not hold their image within My mind, they will evaporate as the solidness of everything You see depends upon My imagination."

Part 6: The Esser Yaad, "So what will happen to all these existing intelligences who have occupied Your present form of imagination?"

The Superconsciousness, "Some of them have to go as I, the architect of the hidden universe, decided to change the sequence of My imagination and change the outcome of this realistic dream."

Part 7: The Esser Yaad, "So why did You intend to change the sequence of Your imagination?"

The Superconsciousness, "Changing the sequence of imagination was part of My strategical advancement. It is like taking one step further towards the completion of what I call necessary."

Part 8: The Esser Yaad, "What is necessary?"

The Superconsciousness, "Projecting the new particles of thought in the image of the sandstorm."

The Esser Yaad, "What is the significance of the sand-storm?"

The Superconsciousness, "The sandstorm has a multitude of significances, so I hereby explain two important reasons of its existence: first, it regenerates My universal power to prepare the thought for the future strategy of creation; and second, it has the ultimate effect of energy to stop the diffusing emptiness."

Part 9: The Esser Yaad, "How do You intend to stop the diffusing emptiness?"

The Superconsciousness, "Through the solidness of My voice."

The Esser Yaad, "How do You utilise the solidness of Your voice?"

The Superconsciousness, "By the recitation of the certain words of power."

The Esser Yaad, "What mystical words of power do You recite?"

The Superconsciousness, "I recite one of the alpha letters of the Oracle."

The Esser Yaad, "How do You recite this alpha letter of the Oracle?"

The Superconsciousness, "Holding the might of the first universal magic within My mind, I utter the words of power in this manner of recitation: 'Cease! Expansion cease. Expansion is enough. Enough is enough!' "

INTRODUCTION TO CHAPTER 4
THE MATRIX OF THE DEEP SLEEP

The conversation continues. The Esser Yaad feels that there is a conflict ahead, waiting to challenge His existing power of fire. He regards this conflict as the path to prevent the catastrophe and control the totality of the third universe. In this conversation, the Esser Yaad expresses His deepest concern. He majestically declares that He is the solidness and absolute reality that exists within the mind of the Superconsciousness, meaning that He cannot be eliminated. The elimination of the Esser Yaad would mean the elimination of any possibility. Then the Esser Yaad explains that by the destruction of fire within the mind, the atmosphere would freeze, the biochemical temperature of the brain would deteriorate and the mind would enter the state of 'Mink', the void of motionless complexity.

Then the Esser Yaad continues and says that He cannot and should not be exterminated as He is the ocean of thought and His extermination would change the activities of the brain. The brain without the Esser would not exercise the resisting cells of construction, and by time, the mind would collapse and fall into the state of oblivion. There He opens the new gate, explaining the oblivion as the matrix of the deep sleep, the deep sleep with the illusionary sensation of dream.

Now, are we in this state of matrix? Is life just a long dream? Is it the imagination without the solidness of reality? It is up to us to activate the ocean of Esser within our minds and recog-

nise that we live in the reality, the reality within the mind of the Superconsciousness.

Follow the path of the Exordium. The Exordium is the new concept of philosophy.

———————————

CHAPTER FOUR

THE MATRIX OF THE DEEP SLEEP

Part 1: As this mysterious dialogue is constructing the future philosophy of the Exordium and the hidden history of the universe, we begin to follow the rest of this conversation as it really took place, before the existence of conventional time.

Part 2: The Superconsciousness continued, "I was monitoring Your every motion, Your every word and Your every thought. You have done well. Through the magic of moisture, You have broken the offensive pattern of My dynamic sandstorm. Now, what do You think is going to emerge?"

The Esser Yaad, "The eventuality of yet another conflict."

The Superconsciousness, "Conflict?"

The Esser Yaad, "Yes, another conflict to prevent the catastrophe of elimination and control the totality of the universe."

The Superconsciousness, "Which universe?"

The Esser Yaad, "The third universe."

Part 3: The Superconsciousness, "Esser Yaad, what are You going to do? As You know, I have decided to evaporate certain existing characters from My central brain. My intention is to replace them with a new and different series of imagination."

The Esser Yaad, "You can eliminate every existing character from Your central brain, but trying to eliminate Me is like pressing the most self-destructive mechanism of all."

The Superconsciousness, "Why?"

The Esser Yaad, "There are many mysterious reasons behind this sophisticated matter of thought."

Part 4: The Superconsciousness, "Explain the first one."

The Esser Yaad, "I am the solidness of Your imagination. Only through the effectiveness of My power can You sit above the throne of excellence."

The Superconsciousness, "Explain the second one."

The Esser Yaad, "I am the ultimate manifestation of fire. Eliminating the fire would create two negative regions of deterioration. First, it would form the void of the freezing atmosphere; and second, it would construct the massive vortex."

Part 5: The Superconsciousness, "What is the destructive significance of the freezing atmosphere?"

The Esser Yaad, "The biochemical temperature will deteriorate."

The Superconsciousness, "Biochemical temperature?"

The Esser Yaad, "Yes, the biochemical temperature of the brain."

The Superconsciousness, "What would be the effect of this deterioration?"

The Esser Yaad, "The consciousness would lose the vitality of heat and become the pointless globe of freezing intensity."

Part 6: The Superconsciousness, "What is the name of this pointless globe of freezing intensity?"

The Esser Yaad, "The state of 'Mink'. "

The Superconsciousness, "What is the state of Mink?"

The Esser Yaad, "It is the moment when the brain ceases to function and becomes the empty frame of motionless complexity."

Part 7: The Superconsciousness, "What kind of condition can be caused by the massive vortex that You have mentioned?"

The Esser Yaad, "The force-field of this massive gravity will confuse every resisting cell of the active mind."

The Superconsciousness, "Which resisting cells of the active mind?"

The Esser Yaad, "Those resisting cells that are automatically exercising the very base of the central brain."

Part 8: The Superconsciousness, "What is the effect of this confusion?"

The Esser Yaad, "It magnetically pulls every consciousness and every future intelligence into the state of oblivion."

The Superconsciousness, "What is the state of oblivion?"

The Esser Yaad, "It is the matrix of the deep sleep, the deep sleep with the illusionary sensation of dream."

INTRODUCTION TO CHAPTER 5
THE REALITY OF THE ABSOLUTE

Now the Superconsciousness expresses His satisfaction that out of His original form of thoughtfulness has emerged a character that is impossible to defeat. The Superconsciousness continues to explain that the Esser Yaad is the reality of His thought. Through the existence of the Esser Yaad, all His imagination would turn into reality and every aspect of His dream would come true.

In this chapter, the Esser Yaad asks the Superconsciousness what is the intention of His dream. As we are going to read, the intention of His dream is to create the reality of the absolute. The Esser Yaad represents the formation, the ultimate certitude, the certitude of intelligence. Why? Because the Esser Yaad, through the practicality of His mysticism, created His own image out of the flames of fire, the image that represents the structure of oneness (the origin of beginning).

The conversation continues as the Superconsciousness asks the Esser Yaad how He transformed Himself into His present form of mystery. Even though He knows the answer, He wants the Esser Yaad to enlighten the inhabitants of the world. The answer is most unusual. He says that He transformed His image through the ultimate magic of fire.

The Superconsciousness asks what is this magic of fire. The Esser Yaad begins to explain His definition of magic. He says that magic is power. Which power? The power of transformation, the power to create the cause and control the effect. He says that magic is the capability to put in use the words of wonder. To Him, magic is the hidden instrument of resurrection and the shield against the demon of decay and the process of extermination. He says that magic is the concept of influence, changing the height of any imagination into reality.

Now is the time to learn and follow the path of this magic. We have to conquer every altitude of this wisdom so we can perform the impossible and create a metaphysical image of ourselves. This means we can resurrect from the tightness of our graves and enter into the new dimension of life, the everlasting immortality.

Does it mean we can break the illusion of death and touch the legendary tree of life? Yes, the Exordium contains every branch of this sacred tree. Its secrets, if mastered, will take you beyond any existing phenomena. Believe me, it is real. It is possible. It is the possibility that is certain.

CHAPTER FIVE

THE REALITY OF THE ABSOLUTE

Part 1: This chapter is another series of celestial philosophy. I, Mehdi Zand, the constructive manifestation of the divine force of fire, take you into yet another episode of mystery. I take you into the moment when the Superconsciousness and the Esser Yaad are constructing the passages of wisdom in the format of one of the most enigmatic conversations of all. Now we enter this historical scene as the Superconsciousness continues.

Part 2: The Superconsciousness, "It is interesting."

The Esser Yaad, "What is interesting?"

The Superconsciousness, "It is interesting that out of My imagination was raised the character that is impossible to defeat."

The Esser Yaad, "I hope You are pleased with this outcome."

The Superconsciousness, "I am pleased. I know in future every scene of My imagination would turn into reality and the solidness of My dream would come true."

Part 3: The conversation between the Superconsciousness and the Esser Yaad continues:

The Esser Yaad, "What did You imagine?"

The Superconsciousness, "To create."

The Esser Yaad, "To create what?"

The Superconsciousness, "To create the reality."

The Esser Yaad, "What reality?"

The Superconsciousness, "The reality of the absolute."

The Esser Yaad, "What is the reality of the absolute?"

The Superconsciousness, "The formation of My cosmic image."

Part 4: The Esser Yaad, "What do You mean?"

The Superconsciousness, "I mean that I have constructed the first manifestation of power."

The Esser Yaad, "Does it mean that I represent the totality of Your imagination?"

The Superconsciousness, "Yes. From the moment that You left the centre of My fire, I knew that the first constructive division of positivity had begun."

The Esser Yaad, "So what did You think of the moment when I penetrated the heart of emptiness to search for the solid ground of stability?"

The Superconsciousness, "My thought was flourishing with virtual dreams. Since the time of Your necessary exodus, I was monitoring Your constructive advancement towards the reality of the golden destination, the divinity."

Part 5: The Superconsciousness continues, "Esser Yaad, what was Your original reaction when You saw the mysterious image of the unknown, the image in the far distance of the emptiness, the image of magic that I wanted You to resemble, the image that sustained the height of celestial eliteness?"

The Esser Yaad, "When I saw this mysterious image of certainty, I became attentively thoughtful."

The Superconsciousness, "Why?"

The Esser Yaad, "I realised the new era of existence and the new cycle of life had begun."

The Superconsciousness, "Your transfiguration into this embodiment of fire was excellent. You have definitely duplicated the exactness of this metaphysical image. You certainly did conquer the totality of the first universe. But tell Me, how did You transform Yourself into this present form of mystery?"

The Esser Yaad, "Through the celestial and ultimate magic of fire."

The Superconsciousness, "I know that I am connected to every depth and every altitude of this magic, but how do You define the magic of fire?"

Part 6: The Esser Yaad, "To Me, as I am the founder of practical mysticism, magic is the power. Magic is the knowledge. Magic is the strategy to create the cause and control the effect. To Me, magic is the hidden letters of wonder that encompasses any chosen field of the universal existence. I know magic is My voice of resurrection. It is the seal of power against the process of decay and the demon of extermination. Do You know what I think

magic really is? Magic is the concept of influence trans-
forming the height of My imagination into the domain
of reality."

The Superconsciousness, "Does Your magic influence
the sequence of the hidden future?"

The Esser Yaad, "Yes. My magic is the ultimate path of
recognition. It is the instrument of light to construct
the passage to everlasting existence. It is the vehicle of
hidden fire to mould the unwritten phases of destiny.
My magic penetrates into the foundation of every
universal law."

INTRODUCTION TO CHAPTER 6
THE MIND IS THE MOST POWERFUL
MECHANISM OF INFLUENCE

In this chapter, the Esser Yaad explains to the reader of the Exordium that the will is the origin of regenerating energy, and the mind, the most powerful mechanism of influence. What does this mean? It means that through the existence of the will and the magical sophistication of the mind, creation can be achieved.

In this episode, the Superconsciousness asks the Esser Yaad to name some of the procedures of His universal magic of fire. The Esser Yaad names the first procedure as invocation[1] and the second procedure as incantation[2]. The Esser Yaad continues and explains the third procedure as the interplanetary connection. It means through the practicality of His magic, one can enter into any existing dimension. But remember, as the Esser Yaad says, the most important factor is the mind. We have to exercise our intellect. We have to regenerate our will. This is the only way to break the era of unthoughtfulness and enter the new time of planetary evolution.

So be it.

_____

[1] Invocation: calling upon certain entities or powers
[2] Incantation: repeating words of power for magical purposes

The Mind Is The Most Powerful Mechanism Of Influence

Part 1: As the conversation regarding the reality of magic was reaching the ultimate point of conclusion, I, Mehdi Zand, the manifestation of the constructive fire of thought, take you once again into the centre of the most gigantic brain of existence, the region where this mysterious conversation continued as follows.

Part 2: The Superconsciousness, "So You transformed Yourself from the flames of fire into this image of divine intelligence. But tell Me, how many practical procedures does your magic contain?"

The Esser Yaad, "My magic encompasses many practical procedures of fire."

The Superconsciousness, "Are these practical procedures easy to comprehend?"

The Esser Yaad, "No, they are beyond the normal state of comprehension."

The Superconsciousness, "Can you enlighten the inhabitants of the world as to what is the effect of your magic upon the element of consciousness?"

The Esser Yaad, "Yes. Through the magic of fire, consciousness can reach to the level of cosmic awareness."

The Superconsciousness, "Cosmic awareness?"

The Esser Yaad, "Yes, the cosmic awareness has many celestial advantages."

The Superconsciousness, "Can you name one of the advantages of this cosmic awareness?"

The Esser Yaad, "Yes. Telepathical transmission."

The Superconsciousness, "Can you name another?"

The Esser Yaad, "Yes. Telethought communication."

The Superconsciousness, "Can you name yet another advantage of this cosmic awareness?"

The Esser Yaad, "Yes. Pictographic projection."

Part 3: The Superconsciousness, "Is there any contacting equation within Your practical mysticism of fire?"

The Esser Yaad, "Yes, there are many contacting equations in My universal magic of fire."

The Superconsciousness, "Can You enlighten the inhabitants of the world as to one of these contacting procedures of fire?"

The Esser Yaad, "Yes. Invocation."

The Superconsciousness, "What is invocation?"

The Esser Yaad, "Invocation can be explained as calling upon a certain form of intelligence to manifest, either in the metaphysical plane or future physical dimensions."

Part 4: The conversation between the Superconsciousness and the Esser Yaad still continues:

The Superconsciousness, "Would You name another connecting procedure of Your universal magic of fire?"

The Esser Yaad, "Yes, the process of incantation."

The Superconsciousness, "What is the nature of incantation?"

The Esser Yaad, "Incantation is to repeat certain words of the Oracle in the perfect mode of sequence."

The Superconsciousness, "Which oracle?"

The Esser Yaad, "The only Oracle. The Oracle of Incipience."

Part 5: The Superconsciousness, "Can You name yet another contacting equation of Your universal magic of fire?"

The Esser Yaad, "Yes. The interplanetary connection."

The Superconsciousness, "What does the interplanetary connection mean?"

The Esser Yaad, "It means utilising certain letters of power in conjunction with the geometrical images of mystery as the gate."

The Superconsciousness, "As the gate?"

The Esser Yaad, "Yes, as the gate to enter any planetary dimension."

The Superconsciousness, "What would be the significance of entering other dimensions?"

The Esser Yaad, "To see and experience other forms of intelligence(s)."

Part 6: The Superconsciousness, "Esser Yaad, what is the most complex achievement that can be attained by Your magic?"

The Esser Yaad, "Creation."

The Superconsciousness, "As You are the creator of mysticism, what are the most important factors in Your practice of fire?"

The Esser Yaad, "There are many important factors."

The Superconsciousness, "Name the first important factor."

The Esser Yaad, "The mind."

The Superconsciousness, "What does the mind do?"

The Esser Yaad, "The mind is the most powerful mechanism of influence."

The Superconsciousness, "Can You name the second important factor in this magic?"

The Esser Yaad, "Yes. The endurance of the will."

The Superconsciousness, "What is the advantage of the will in this concept of mystery?"

The Esser Yaad, "The will is the genesis of regeneration."

The Superconsciousness, "Regeneration of what?"

The Esser Yaad, "Regeneration of the energy."

INTRODUCTION TO CHAPTER 7
I AM THE MIND OF FIRE

As the conversation between the Superconsciousness and the Lord of constructive fire continues, the Esser Yaad reveals yet another type of mystical knowledge by which He can construct and adorn the world of Esser Yaad.

In this chapter, He says that magic is the instrument to create His souls of fire. But who are the souls of fire? He says the souls of fire are those who would become the solid foundation of constructive reality. Basically, the souls of fire are those who hold the essence of thoughtfulness within every particle of their existence. The Esser Yaad emphasises that these souls of fire are always loyal to the first and second creator of the existing universe. Let us see; who is the first creator? The Superconsciousness, the cause of genesis. Who is the second creator? The cause of the Exordium, the mind of fire. As the Esser Yaad says, He is the mind of fire.

In the next part of this conversation, the Superconsciousness questions the Esser Yaad as to what He intends to do with His universal wisdom of fire. The Esser Yaad says that He wants to teach this art of mystery to His selected souls so they can exercise their minds and discover their spiritual capabilities. In this conversation, the Esser Yaad mentions the reality of the keys, the keys of consciousness.

Now, do you possess the qualities that the Esser Yaad mentions? Are you searching for the nature of the hidden light? Do you contemplate upon the patterns of life? Do you want to raise your consciousness? Are you a soul of fire? Well, I am. I am a soul of fire. I have discovered the tree of life through the magic of Yaad. Yes, I am going to recreate my metaphysical body. I am going to resurrect and cross the land of the dead. Are you going to follow me? Or are you going to stay behind? I hold the seventy-seven keys of universal consciousness. I am ready to present them to whoever wishes to conquer his inner-self and touch the fire of immortality.

So let it be written.

Let it be heard.

CHAPTER SEVEN

I AM THE MIND OF FIRE

Part 1: The time was passing inaccurately and inconsistently. The Esser Yaad was still standing firm in the centre of the most gigantic brain of the universe. The conversation between these two mighty forces of the unseen was getting deeper and deeper to the ultimate point of glory. We enter into yet another series of this conversation as the Superconsciousness continues His mystical and peaceful interrogation in this manner of discourse.

Part 2: The Superconsciousness, "What do You intend to do with this unique type of universal wisdom?"

The Esser Yaad, "To construct and to magnify the world of Esser Yaad."

The Superconsciousness, "How do You magnify the world of Esser Yaad?"

The Esser Yaad, "By creating the souls."

The Superconsciousness, "Creating the souls? What kind of souls?"

The Esser Yaad, "The souls of fire."

The Superconsciousness, "Who are the souls of fire?"

The Esser Yaad, "The souls of fire are those images who become the solid foundation of constructive thoughtfulness."

The Superconsciousness, "How do they become the solid foundation of constructive thoughtfulness?"

The Esser Yaad, "Through the essence that I project into the very centre of their existence."

Part 3: The Superconsciousness, "What kind of essence do You project into the very centre of their existence?"

The Esser Yaad, "The essence that I project has many qualities of life."

The Superconsciousness, "Can You name three of these qualities of life?"

The Esser Yaad, "Yes. The first is the quality to search for the core of existence and the urge to discover the root of immortality. The second is the quality to contemplate upon the patterns of life and the dedication to raise the intelligence to the ultimate point of perfection. And the third is the quality to be loyal to the first and the second creator, as well as standing against the nature of anti-matter consciousness."

Part 4: The Superconsciousness, "Who is the first creator?"

The Esser Yaad, "The cause of genesis."

The Superconsciousness, "Who is the cause of genesis?"

The Esser Yaad, "You are the cause of genesis."

The Superconsciousness, "Who is the second creator?"

The Esser Yaad, "The mind of fire."

The Superconsciousness, "Who is this mind of fire?"

The Esser Yaad, "I am the mind of fire."

Part 5: The Superconsciousness, "What else do You intend to do with Your universal wisdom of mystery?"

The Esser Yaad, "I will teach certain aspects of this art to My selected souls of fire."

The Superconsciousness, "Why?"

The Esser Yaad, "So they can assist and carry out the positive programming."

The Superconsciousness, "Which positive programming?"

The Esser Yaad, "The positive programming of the mind exorcitation."

The Superconsciousness, "How can they assist and carry out this positive programming?"

The Esser Yaad, "By learning My ultimate philosophy and exercising the practical section of this mysterious concept of awakening."

The Superconsciousness, "How would You differentiate the inner capabilities of Your souls?"

The Esser Yaad, "In accordance with their intelligence and their superiority."

The Superconsciousness, "How do You classify their superiority?"

The Esser Yaad, "By the number of keys they obtain."

The Superconsciousness, "Which keys?"

The Esser Yaad, "The keys of consciousness."

Part 6: The Superconsciousness, "Can You elaborate briefly?"

The Esser Yaad, "Yes. Through the positive programming of exorcitation, through conquering the zone of every key, they can activate the chemistry of their hidden brain to the point of cosmic awareness."

Introduction to Chapter 8
The Transformation Of My Virtual Dream

This chapter should be read thoughtfully as the Supercon-sciousness explains the reason behind the changing of His realistic dream. As to how He is going to alter His realistic dream, the Superconsciousness continues by saying that He will slowly and forcefully hover above this spreading region of emptiness. He will then enlarge His very self and descend upon His imagination. By doing this, He will ultimately encompass every necessary lowland and the height of every altitude.

It is strange to hear that the Superconsciousness magnifies His hidden image and lands upon the surface of His own imagi-nation, is it not? But He does this to eliminate every insignificant and unfocused thought-form in this domain of emptiness. How-ever, the most important reason is that He knows the pattern(s) of creation are on their way, so He encompasses His own dream and conquers His imagination, allowing the ultimate possibility to manifest.

Now we reach one of the philosophical masterpieces of the Exordium. You might have heard the name 'Underworld'. The Egyptians talked about it, the Greeks have mentioned it and you can hear this name in Indian theology and in many other existing philosophies. But no one has explained how or why the Underworld was formed, no one has realised or revealed that the Superconsciousness magnified His image and landed upon His imagination so the world could be created beneath the solidness of His image. Listen to His historical declaration:

"It is essential to understand that every notable and future character, or whatever has to manifest and become a solid foundation of reality, should be created and personified beneath My metaphysical embodiment."

What does this mean? It means the Superconsciousness, with this strange manoeuvre, laid upon His own dream and so allowed the Esser Yaad to create a new world. As this new world was directly beneath the hidden image of the Godhead, it was named the 'Underworld'.

This new doctrine of philosophy has been discovered by myself, the writer of the Exordium. I have travelled ethereally; I have gone beyond the ultimate point of thoughtfulness and have seen what really took place before the birth of the physical universe. From this aeon of golden memory, I have become a part of history as the first soul of fire who has revealed what was concealed, who has defined what was indefinable and who has unfolded what was hidden. I, Mehdi Zand, present a new definition and the real reason behind the formation of the most enigmatic and legendary region of all: the Underworld.

Now let us read the chapter and feel the actual declaration of the Superconsciousness, or the Godhead, regarding the construction of this mystical domain of existence. Let us proceed.

CHAPTER EIGHT

THE TRANSFORMATION OF
MY VIRTUAL DREAM

Part 1: In this chapter, we enter the moment when the Superconsciousness, after a very short aeon of silence, continued His mysterious conversation in this manner of discourse.

Part 2: The Superconsciousness, "Excellent! I knew that I had invested correctly in Your wisdom. But do You know the actual reason behind the transformation of My virtual dream?"

The Esser Yaad, "Yes, but for future reference, You should enlighten this historical matter accordingly."

The Superconsciousness, "Whatever I say, it should be written, it should be uttered, it should be heard. There are three main reasons behind this inevitable transformation:

"First, the emptiness was the original base of the imagination. It was a testing zone to see the growth of My inner characteristic; but after a very short aeon of inconsistent time, it began to diffuse with the ultimate velocity. Its diffusion broke the boundary of every domain of thought. It was beginning to spread endlessly. So I concentrated and recognised the fact that the only way to sustain the emptiness was to enlarge my hidden image to equal the size of this emptiness and then rise to the highest point of the existing altitude, the horizon."

Part 3: The Superconsciousness continued,

"In the next stage, I will slowly, but forcefully, hover above and then lie upon this diffusing region to encompass the height of the unseen and every lowland in this void of emptiness.

"I know this mystical interface between My metaphysical embodiment and My imagination will cause a certain pressure to emerge and the darkness to appear, but this is the only way to envelop the totality of My dream and obstruct the expansion of emptiness."

Part 4: The Superconsciousness still continued and explained the second reason behind this transformation:

The Superconsciousness, "The second reason behind this necessary transformation was to clear My central brain from all the thought-forms that had become insignificant, unfocused and cluttered through the passing age of inconsistent time. To be able to carry out this self-appointed mission, I began to activate every circuit of thoughtfulness to construct the new fusion of electric particles of mind in the image of the sandstorm."

Part 5: The Superconsciousness still continued, "I am aware that the power of this sandstorm will eliminate certain existing characters from the path of future history, but in order to cleanse the centre of My mind from every intrusive image, this procedure of electric purification is necessary."

Part 6: The Superconsciousness continued and explained the third reason behind the transformation of His virtual dream in this manner of discourse:

The Superconsciousness, "Now the third and the most important reason behind this inevitable transformation: I am the root of existence and the totality of what would be recognised as the world. It is essential to understand that every notable and future character, or whatever has to manifest and become a solid foundation of reality, should be created and personified beneath My metaphysical embodiment.

"They should become the existing inhabitants within the boundary of this new land, the region of intensified pressure. So, as You can see, this would be the birth and the emergence of the most enigmatic and legendary region of existence: the Underworld."

Introduction to Chapters 9-11

Underworld. The Esser Yaad hears the word 'Underworld'. He immediately begins to strategise. He knows that He is invincible, but what about the particles of emptiness? He says that He cannot sit aside and witness the elimination of these intelligences, especially those who have become a part of His universal alliance.

In these coming chapters, the Superconsciousness says that through the descent of His hidden form, He will encompass the depths of His imagination (His realistic dream). After this declaration, He continues and asks if the Esser Yaad realises what would happen when He descends and lands upon His imagination. The Esser Yaad says yes, the darkness. So what could the Esser Yaad do? Here, yet again, is another philosophical masterpiece, the new concept concerning the emergence of the gods, creation and the Underworld.

The Esser Yaad explains the solution: an unimaginable procedure of magic. He says that He will project Himself out of the mind of the Superconsciousness. Imagine that. Where would He go? Where is this place? How can the Esser Yaad transport Himself into any place where there is no presence of the Godhead? That is a mystery, the mystery that is only known to the Esser Yaad, and the Esser Yaad alone.

But He carries on. He takes the mysticism further. He says that He will take a supply of oxygen with Him. What an interesting phenomenon. God needs oxygen? Is this the same oxygen? I say not. This is the oxygen of the hidden world. Possibly this oxygen is one of the instruments of power against the cycle of time and its touchable effect, the age.

In the forthcoming chapters, the Esser Yaad explains more about this place that He transports Himself into, the place that has no name and no recognisation of existence. This domain is beyond the frontier of any thought. It is above the height of any form of imagination. It was beyond my imagination too, until one day, the light shone upon my heart. My mind opened and the secret of the hidden universe was revealed into the totality of my being. My mind was taken into the dimension beyond the conventional time.

Do you know what I saw? Step-by-step, I saw the entire scenario that the Esser Yaad describes to create this Underworld. Although you are going to discover the creation of this domain through the future chapters of the Exordium, nevertheless, let me explain what I saw. Remember, if people think this is blasphemy, let them think it. If people say this is imagination, let them say it. I know what I saw. I know what I did. I went beyond the depths of any patterns of concentration to bring forth what you, the sons of Man, are about to read. Read and judge for yourself.

Through my inner vision, I could see this domain that had no recognition of existence. I could see that this place had no gravity, no oxygen, no hydrogen. The eyes of intelligence could not survive and the thought-forms of Hee'yaak would evaporate the moment they entered this sphere of the unknown. Nevertheless, I concentrated thoughtfully to see the rest of this mysterious operation.

I saw the Esser Yaad standing in the image of outstretched divinity. He was looking directly into the mind of the Superconsciousness. He was outside the solidness of this imagination. Then I saw the most unbelievable and unusual procedure of magic. I saw the Esser Yaad standing in front of the imaginary altar of fire. I saw Him magnify His hidden form to equal the size of this imagination. I saw Him reach out His magical hands of power and stretch the outer layers of this imagination downwards. Yes, by doing so, He constructed the domain in the image of a perfect geometrical hemisphere. This was the formation and structure of the Underworld.

So read these three chapters, imagine the situation and get the most benefit out of these golden pages of mystery.

So be it.

Chapter Nine

It Has No Recognition
Of Existence

Part 1: After the explanation by the Superconsciousness regarding the birth of the Underworld, the Esser Yaad concentrated thoughtfully and formulated yet another highly mysterious conversation in this manner of discourse.

Part 2: The Esser Yaad, "Did You say the Underworld?"

The Superconsciousness, "Yes. As it would be positioned directly beneath the world that I represent, it shall be called the Underworld."

Part 3: Then the Esser Yaad, this constructive manifestation of the Superconsciousness, changed the sequence of the conversation and said,

"Time, however inconsistent, is against the very core of My essence. The sandstorm is reaching the end of the emptiness. Soon, certain particles of this region will be eliminated as though they had never existed before. I cannot sit aside and witness the elimination of every intelligence of emptiness, especially those who have become a part of My universal alliance."

Part 4: Then the Superconsciousness raised His eloquent voice of mystery and questioned the Esser Yaad in this manner of presentation:

The Superconsciousness, "Esser Yaad, do You know the effect that would follow the interface between My metaphysical image and the depths of My imagination?"

The Esser Yaad, "Yes. Darkness there would be."

The Superconsciousness, "Excellent. Well observed. But how do You know there would be darkness?"

The Esser Yaad, "It is inevitable. If You lie upon Your imagination and Your hidden image equals the size of its perimeter, there would be no space for anything else other than darkness."

Part 5: The Superconsciousness, "Esser Yaad, do You realise that when My hidden image totally encompasses every surface of emptiness, there would be no space for any inhabitant to survive?"

The Esser Yaad, "Yes, I am aware that there would be no space between Your hidden image and the depths of Your imagination. At this moment of inconsistent time, I am calculating the intensity of the atmosphere and the pressure of the situation."

Part 6. The Superconsciousness, "Do You think You can survive the intensity of the atmosphere, the pressure of the situation, and, simultaneously, be a saviour for the particles of emptiness?"

The Esser Yaad, "Yes, I will search to stretch the layers of Your imagination and create the gap."

The Superconsciousness, "Which gap?"

The Esser Yaad, "The gap in the midst of Your imagination."

The Superconsciousness, "Why do You intend to create a gap in the midst of My imagination?"

The Esser Yaad, "To find the opening."

The Superconsciousness, "What is the significance of the opening?"

The Esser Yaad, "So I can project Myself into the region of nothing and nothingness."

Part 7: The Superconsciousness, "What is the name of this region?"

The Esser Yaad, "This region has no name."

The Superconsciousness, "Why does this region have no name?"

The Esser Yaad, "Because it has no recognition of existence."

The Superconsciousness, "Why does this region have no recognition of existence?"

The Esser Yaad, "As it is beyond the frontier of Your thought, it has no recognition of existence."

Chapter Ten

I Have Invested Correctly
In Your Wisdom

Part 1: When the Esser Yaad introduced the region of nothing and nothingness, the Superconsciousness yet again began to interrogate the practicality of the Esser Yaad's magic in this manner of discourse.

Part 2: The Superconsciousness, "What kind of sensation do You think would encompass this region which has no name?"

The Esser Yaad, "This region would have a variety of unusual sensations."

The Superconsciousness, "Like what?"

The Esser Yaad, "There would be no presence of gravity, to start with."

The Superconsciousness, "Is there any other form of sensation?"

The Esser Yaad, "Yes. The absence of the elements of vitality, like hydrogen and oxygen."

The Superconsciousness, "Would there be any sign of the eyes of intelligence?"

The Esser Yaad, "No, absolutely not. The eyes of intelligence can only survive and carry on their mission within the perimeter of Your imagination."

Part 3: The Superconsciousness, "What about the Hee'yaak? Would there be any flow of activity from these intelligences of life?"

The Esser Yaad, "No, even the Hee'yaak would cease to exist within the perimeter of this region."

The Superconsciousness, "Esser Yaad, would there be any formation of solidness in this land?"

The Esser Yaad, "No, there would not be any formation of matter. All I expect is the deep space, the void of absolute nothingness."

The Superconsciousness, "Do You think there would be any evidence of different temperatures in this void of nothingness?"

The Esser Yaad, "No, there would be no difference of temperatures: neither the feeling of heat nor the sensation of coolness."

Part 4: The Superconsciousness, "Esser Yaad, when You have projected Yourself into this region, what would be Your first strategical manoeuvre?"

The Esser Yaad, "As there would be no solid ground of stability, I would have to concentrate and utilise the practicality of magic to create a suitable base beneath My hidden image of fire."

Part 5: The Superconsciousness, "What would be Your second strategical manoeuvre?"

The Esser Yaad, "I would inhale infrequently."

The Superconsciousness, "But there would be no sign of oxygen to inhale. How can You inhale infrequently?"

The Esser Yaad, "I would inhale from the supply of oxygen that I carry in the form of a breathing apparatus."

The Superconsciousness, "Where would You keep this supply of oxygen?"

The Esser Yaad, "I would hold and carry it in the palm of My hand."

The Superconsciousness, "What is the breathing apparatus?"

The Esser Yaad, "It is a system of artificial respiration."

Part 6: The Superconsciousness, "Esser Yaad, what happens next?"

The Esser Yaad, "Next is the most enigmatic and mysterious manoeuvre of all time."

The Superconsciousness, "Why is this manoeuvre the most mysterious procedure of all time?"

The Esser Yaad, "Because if I fail, it would be the end."

The Superconsciousness, "The end of what?"

The Esser Yaad, "The end of the cycle."

The Superconsciousness, "Which cycle?"

The Esser Yaad, "The cycle of existence."

The Superconsciousness, "What is the cycle of existence?"

The Esser Yaad, "The sequence of life."

The Superconsciousness, "Why would Your failure end the sequence of life?"

The Esser Yaad, "Because there would be no solid base for any type of imagination to flourish."

Part 7: The Superconsciousness, "Excellent! It seems that You have contemplated and calculated everything accordingly. As I said before, I have invested correctly in Your wisdom."

CHAPTER ELEVEN

THE FORMATION AND THE STRUCTURE OF THE UNDERWORLD

Part 1: In this chapter, once again we travel into the moment, into the inconsistent time when the Superconsciousness, after a very short aeon of absolute thoughtfulness, continued His mysterious conversation in this manner of discourse.

Part 2: The Superconsciousness, "Esser Yaad, I know that You have mentally prepared Yourself for this highly strategical operation, but how are You going to project Yourself into this domain?"

The Esser Yaad, "I am going to utilise the ultimate procedure of My celestial magic of fire."

The Superconsciousness, "Can You elaborate upon this mysticism for the future reference of universal history?"

Part 3: The Esser Yaad, "Yes. First, I will stand in the position of outstretched divinity, repeating certain words of power to create a shield of protection as the safety of My essence is exceptionally significant. Second, I will concentrate thoughtfully using every ray of My intelligence and every particle of My awareness to imagine Myself above the altar of fire. Third, I will repeat the alpha letters of the Exordium to construct the ground of stability within the height of My imagination. Fourth, I will apply the greatness of My power and transfer the solidness of My being into this ground of stability. And fifth, I will project this ground with Myself in it somewhere outside Your very own imagination, into this domain that has no recognition of existence."

Part 4: The Superconsciousness, "Esser Yaad, is it not detrimental to be outside My virtual dream? It is like You are sacrificing Yourself for this concept of divinity."

The Esser Yaad, "If I stay within the perimeter of Your dream, I will have to struggle endlessly to cease the process of extermination. But if I want to prevail in this conflict of becoming and become the saviour for the particles of emptiness and reach the ultimate pinnacle of My divinity, there is no other choice."

Part 5: The Superconsciousness, "Esser Yaad, when You have successfully projected Your very self outside the perimeter of My mind, what would be Your main strategy?"

The Esser Yaad, "My strategy would consist of three main sections of mystery. First, I would calculate and measure the depths and the lengths of Your imagination. Second, by the magic of self-transfiguration, I would enlarge My hidden image to equal the size of Your virtual dream. And third, by reciting the very letter(s) of My magical utterance, I would reach out My hands of power to stretch the outer layers of Your imagination downwards to construct the domain in the image of a perfect geometrical hemisphere."

Part 6: The Superconsciousness, "What would be the significance of this domain?"

> The Esser Yaad, "As it is directly beneath the solidness of Your hidden form, it would be the formation and the structure of the Underworld."

Introduction to Chapter 12
I Would Formulate
The Path Of The Exodus

When the Esser Yaad explained how He would construct the Underworld, the Superconsciousness asked Him what would be His next plan. This ultimate fire of existence, or the Esser Yaad, explained that He would construct the path, the path of exodus. The path of exodus means that He would somehow create a passage so that every intelligence of emptiness could transfer themselves into this domain, the Underworld. Then the Superconsciousness asks the Esser Yaad about the entrance of the darkness and the strategy that He has to face this element.

In His answer, the Esser Yaad explains yet another brilliant strategy to confront the darkness. He says that He would create some form of atomic rays of electrification with the capability to penetrate the centre of every element and the mind of every inhabitant. What is this enigmatic God talking about? What do these rays of electrification do? The Esser Yaad says they would reflect and transfer the hidden beams of fire so the visibility can manifest. Yes, the Esser Yaad is talking of the emergence, the emergence of sight. The entrance of sight has never been revealed as it is in the book of Exordium. When sight enters the history, the duality of the first kind would emerge: the darkness and the light. It has been said, "Let there be light." This is how the light was formed before the beginning of the touchable universe.

Then the Esser Yaad continues and explains that every energy level depends upon the systematic alteration between *light and darkness. This is also another important subject for the practitioner of the universal magic of fire. Anyone who wants to rise above his original consciousness, reach the height of his intelligence and connect his inner self to the totality of the universe should know how this systematic alteration would work. The Esser Yaad says they work in accordance to the changing cycles of time.*

Let us read the chapter and enjoy the conversation between the two mighty souls of the universe: the first creator, the Super-consciousness, and the Lord of constructive fire, the Esser Yaad.

———————————

CHAPTER TWELVE

I WOULD FORMULATE
THE PATH OF THE EXODUS

Part 1: When the Esser Yaad, this ultimate fire of the Exordium, had explained how He would form the structure and the formation of the Underworld, the Superconsciousness paused for a very short aeon of inconsistent time. Then, full of attentiveness, He raised His voice of eloquence and began the next series of conversations in this manner of discourse.

Part 2: The Superconsciousness, "After the formation of this domain, what would be Your next strategical plan?"

The Esser Yaad, "I would formulate the path of the exodus."

The Superconsciousness, "Why would You formulate the path of this exodus?"

The Esser Yaad, "So every particle of emptiness, especially those who have become part of the universal alliance, can enter this domain and find their second phase of existence."

Part 3: The Superconsciousness, "What would be the benefit of this mystical transference?"

The Esser Yaad, "It would give these intelligences the new degree of life."

The Superconsciousness, "The new degree of life? Can You elaborate on this?"

> The Esser Yaad, "Yes. The new life would give every particle of emptiness a chance to proceed so they can continue their selected patterns of life. If they search for final evolution, it will present them with the opportunity to raise their consciousness within the world that I will construct."

Part 4: The Superconsciousness, "What about the darkness? You know the intensity, the heaviness and the pressure of My hidden image would impose the sensation of darkness upon the atmosphere of this domain that you wish to create."

> The Esser Yaad, "Yes, I am well aware that the pressure and the heaviness of Your image would impose the sentiment of darkness."

The Superconsciousness, "Any strategy to produce the sensation of sight and the degree of visibility?"

> The Esser Yaad, "Yes. I will construct some sort of atomic rays of electrification."

Part 5: The Superconsciousness, "What would be the important factor of these atomic rays of electrification?"

> The Esser Yaad, "These atomic rays will have many dynamic capabilities."

The Superconsciousness, "Can You introduce one of these dynamic capabilities?"

The Esser Yaad, "Yes. By their static influence, they will clear the path for sight and create the power of vision."

The Superconsciousness, "How could they create the power of vision?"

The Esser Yaad, "Through the constant and dynamic pressure."

The Superconsciousness, "Esser Yaad, can You elaborate?"

The Esser Yaad, "Yes. Through the dynamic pressure, these atomic rays of electrification would penetrate the minds of the inhabitants."

Part 6: The Superconsciousness, "Why should they penetrate the minds of the inhabitants?"

The Esser Yaad, "So they can reflect and transform their beams of fire to construct the sensation of visibility."

The Superconsciousness, "Can You explain another aspect of these dynamic capabilities?"

The Esser Yaad, "Yes. They will alternate the situation so every energy level can decrease and increase systematically."

The Superconsciousness, "Systematically?"

The Esser Yaad, "Yes. Systematically, this alteration would distribute the energy transference."

The Superconsciousness, "How does this distribution occur?"

The Esser Yaad, "In accordance with the changing cycles of time."

Part 7: The Superconsciousness, "Excellent. You have proven time after time that You are the completeness of My hidden characteristics. I want You to conquer the totality of the third universe. I want You to sit upon the golden throne of divinity and I want You to become the saviour for every particle of emptiness. But Esser Yaad, as I want You to proceed in this mission of supremacy, I will give You a certain amount of inconsistent time."

Part 8: The Esser Yaad, "When will the countdown of this joint operation begin?"

The Superconsciousness, "The moment when We finish this enlightening conversation."

The Esser Yaad, "How much of this inconsistent time do I have to proceed with My strategy of creation?"

The Superconsciousness, "Your inconsistent time will begin the second that I start to enlarge the totality of My image and will finish precisely at the point when My hidden embodiment equals the size of My imagination."

Introduction to Chapter 13
The Wavelengths Of Understanding

In this chapter, the Esser Yaad follows the procedure of His strategy. Upon the altar of fire, He recites certain words of power and transfers Himself outside the mind of the Superconsciousness, the Godhead. This is the important factor of this episode. How can anything, any being, transfer himself outside the reality of the world? If the Superconsciousness is the reality, then the Esser Yaad, through His magic, steps outside the reality, somewhere that no one can explain.

What is the meaning of this concept? Where does He go? It means He breaks all the barriers of thought, every obstacle of mystery; and He separates Himself for a very short amount of time from the actual meaning and solidness of existence. He goes beyond the boundaries of life. He finds Himself in front of the most gigantic mind of the universe: the mind that creates every reality, the mind that formulates every possibility. He is looking at this ultimate consciousness that no eye has ever seen nor will ever witness again. In this domain of the unknown, the eyes of this Lord of fire, the visual power of the Esser Yaad, are gazing at the centre of this unimaginable wonder: the electrochemical brain of the universe, the inner mind of the Superconsciousness.

Then He says that it is impossible to explain the glory of this sight as the letters cannot contain the greatness of its dynamic sophistication. But He remembers the future as time is simultaneous to Him. He wants every generation to know everything about His quest to divinity. So He says that He can

211

see the thought-forms gathering in many places, then they evaporate and are replaced by the more defined imagination. (We should notice that 'thought-forms' can mean elements, entities or intelligences, or even humans.) More than that, He begins to explain the wavelengths of comprehension. He sees the actual formation of the intelligence.

Is this another case of blasphemy? The Lord God facing the Godhead. The mind of fire standing in front of the ultimate circuit of thoughtfulness, the brain of the Superconsciousness. Can you imagine this phenomenon? Can you visualise the Esser Yaad gazing at this inner motivation of the universe? Can you understand the greatness of this close encounter? What do you think the Esser Yaad can see? Can you feel what He feels?

Read the Exordium. The Exordium is the new concept of philosophy.

CHAPTER THIRTEEN

THE WAVELENGTHS
OF UNDERSTANDING

Part 1: After the last mysterious statement by the Superconsciousness, or the main concentrated intelligence, a heavy silence encompassed the domain of this close encounter.

Part 2: The next stage of history began when the Superconsciousness proceeded to enlarge His hidden image and the Esser Yaad hastened to conquer yet another quest of mystery.

Part 3: Then the Esser Yaad, this ultimate fire of the Exordium, stood in the position of outstretched divinity. He repeated magical words of power and created a shield of protection to safeguard His dynamic essence. As He had strategised, He began to inhale the golden rays of oxygen into the very centre of His heart for the future application of the breathing apparatus.

Part 4: As time was passing inconsistently, this manifestation of constructive fire concentrated in the ultimate mode of thoughtfulness. He used every ray of His dynamic intelligence and every atomic particle of His cosmic awareness and visualised Himself above the altar of fire.

Part 5: When He completed this procedure of visualisation, He repeated certain words of magic, constructed the very domain of stability in His imagination and transferred Himself into the midst of this domain.

Part 6: As the Esser Yaad, our celestial fire of Exordium, knew that the time was against the core of His essence, He contemplated accordingly. He used the power of certain words of mystery and projected this domain (and Himself within it) to somewhere outside the imagination of the Superconsciousness, into the domain that had no recognition of existence.

Part 7: When the Esser Yaad completed every section of His strategical plan, He contemplated attentively and began yet another mystical self-conversation in this manner of discourse:

"I am in the abode of the absolute nothingness. This plane is exactly as I expected it to be."

Lifting His hand from time to time in front of His face to inhale the breath through the texture of His hand, He continued,

"Let Me pause for a very short moment of inconsistent time to see and calculate the greatness of this magnificent mind of existence."

Part 8: The Esser Yaad continued,

"This is above the visualisation of any intelligence. No one has ever seen the totality of this infinite consciousness, and no eyes would ever witness the like of this again. This is unimaginable. It does not matter how hard I try to explain its glory for future reference, the portrayal of this event is impossible as the letters cannot contain the greatness of its dynamic sophistication."

Part 9: After this comment, the Esser Yaad continued His self-conversation in this manner of discourse:

"This is literally the most magnificent metaphysical brain of all time. It is the ultimate chemical circuitry of thoughtfulness that contains every notable and significant eventuality. Let Me look deep into the depths of this absolute centre of electrification. Hmm."

(The sound of His 'Hmm' resonated in every corner of this region that had no recognition of existence.)

"This is the highest instrument of creation. I can see the variety of sophisticated thought-forms gathering in many places. Then they suddenly evaporate only to be replaced by yet another more defined form of imagination. This is the process of replacement and evolution."

Part 10: The Esser Yaad continued His philosophical conversation in this manner of discourse:

"Now I can see the wavelengths of understanding hovering above every domain of this mind to project the sensation of awareness into any existing entity. So this is how the individual intelligence is formed? This is most interesting. It seems that I can increase the level of intelligence by thickening these mystical wavelengths of perception. I should remember to formulate and utilise this technique when I create My souls of fire."

Introduction to Chapter 14
So The Esser Yaad Constructed
The Underworld

Now you are going to enter one of the most magical moments of this book. No man, no philosophy has ever explained why and how the Underworld was formed. They may have talked about the existence of such a place, but no one has explained the strategy behind its creation. With respect to the previous thinkers, philosophers, messengers, prophets and avatars, I, Mehdi Zand, present a new philosophy, a new concept and a new beginning. This is the new beginning to the legend of the gods, their mystery and the formation of their existence.

In this chapter, the Esser Yaad, the Lord of constructive fire, as He had strategised, begins to construct the Underworld. Using the power of His sight, He measures the entire imagination of the Godhead. Then He calculates the height of the altitude and every line of energy that is crossing in the midst of this domain of the unknown.

As this chapter explains, He performs one of the most unbelievable procedures of magic to create the Underworld. He reaches out His hands, stretches the outer layers of the imagination of the Godhead downwards and creates this new domain in the image of a perfect geometrical hemisphere.

Can you imagine that? Do you understand the seriousness of this mystery? What does it mean? Can you visualise the situation in which the Esser Yaad is pulling down the outer layers of the imagination to create the structure of the Under-

world? How can it be possible? How can something or someone be outside the Godhead's mind, let alone perform this supernatural feat? In the beginning of the Exordium, I said that the chapters of this book are written in the specific way so that your imagination can visualise the occurrences of the past. So try to picture the greatness of this event. Use your inner vision and see how the Esser Yaad is standing outside the brain of the Superconsciousness. See in your mind how He stretches out His magical hands of power and pulls the layers of the Godhead's imagination downward to create this mysterious domain that we know as the Underworld.

When the creation of the Underworld is complete, the Esser Yaad projects Himself back into the domain of emptiness to accomplish His self-appointed mission and become the saviour for every particle of emptiness. The procedure of this magic has been written step-by-step in this chapter. Follow His magic of fire and see how the formation and the structure of the Underworld was created. As I said before, no philosophy has ever portrayed the formation of the Underworld in this precise manner. This is the first time, and this honour belongs to the Exordium and the Exordium alone.

So let it be written.

Let it be heard.

CHAPTER FOURTEEN

SO THE ESSER YAAD CONSTRUCTED THE UNDERWORLD

Part 1: In this episode, we travel once more into the moment, into the region of nothing and nothingness, where the Esser Yaad, this fire of existence, was still analysing this ultimate mechanism of thoughtfulness, the mind of the Superconsciousness.

Part 2: As the time passed inaccurately and inconsistently, the Esser Yaad, this manifestation of the Superconsciousness, paused for a very short aeon of silence. Then He raised His volcanic voice of power within the boundaries of this domain and said,

"I can feel the explosion, the eruption. I can notice the constant changes of the progressive cycles of evolution. I can detect the station of the souls of integrity, the domain of the sacred essence of fire and the paradise of the mystical characteristic of glory. I can see the resurrection of the cosmic flames of life, the motivation of every particle of emptiness, and I can see the manifestation of many faces of this universe that are yet to be born."

Part 3: Suddenly, He changed the sequence of His self-conversation in this manner of discourse and said,

"Now I must proceed with the ultimate mode of thoughtfulness to complete My celestial strategy. First, I should concentrate to correctly quantify the depths, the lengths and the intensity of

219

this imagination. I can reach this mystical objective by using the power of My sight to measure the entire lines of energy that are perfectly spread throughout this domain of reality."

Part 4: So He used the inner power of His eyes and measured the depths, the lengths and the intensity of this imagination by calculating every necessary height of altitude and every flickering line of energy.

Part 5: When He had measured the greatness and the size of this imagination, He raised His volcanic voice of power and said,

"This time, I should apply the ultimate procedure of mysticism. I must enlarge My hidden image of fire to equal the size of this imagination and construct the structure of the Underworld.

"This mysterious self-appointed mission can be completed in four different sections of mystery:

"First, to visualise an empty globe of fire.

"Second, I should enlarge the dimensions of this globe to the same size as the virtual imagination of the Superconsciousness.

"Third, I must repeat certain words of power to increase the dimensions of My flesh to the ultimate proportion so I can project Myself into the midst of this globe of fire.

"And the fourth, I have to reach out My hands using the absolute force of energy to stretch the outer layers of the imagination downwards to create this domain in the image of a perfect geometrical hemisphere. When I have successfully accomplished all these celestial objectives, the Underworld will be formulated as it is right beneath the centre of the Superconsciousness."

Part 6: So the Esser Yaad constructed the Underworld once He had completed every section of this strategical manoeuvre. When this geometrical domain was created, He raised His dynamic voice of power once again and said,

"The creation of the Underworld was one of the most significant and sophisticated procedures of all time. I know that within the environment of the Underworld, many constructive faces of fire would emerge. When I was stretching the outer layers of the imagination downwards, I also felt that this zone of mystery could become the first testing zone for many characteristics of the realistic dream to demonstrate their inner capabilities. Either they would rise above their carnal souls[1] or they would disintegrate and fall into the state of oblivion."

Part 7: The Esser Yaad continued,

"Now I should project Myself back into the centre of the imagination so I can proceed with the call of exodus and become the saviour for every particle of emptiness."

Part 8: So the Esser Yaad repeated certain words of the Oracle and transported Himself back into the midst of the realistic dream to fulfil His self-appointed mission and become the saviour for every particle of emptiness. When He returned

---

[1] Carnal soul: the most base and insiinctive part of the human soul

to His region of supremacy, He raised His voice of power and said,

"Now I should utilise My voice of power as a trumpet of salvation and call every intelligence unto Myself so I can construct the path of the exodus and break the seal of the future catastrophe and the talisman of oblivion."

Introduction to Chapters 15-19

So the Esser Yaad, this Lord of constructive fire transfers Himself back into the domain of emptiness. There He creates another celestial melody so every particle can hear His voice of salvation. When this call of salvation is complete, many intelligences gather around Him yet again. With jubilation and excitement, they begin to converse with this force of fire. They ask Him if He had discovered the cause of the sandstorm. The conversation carries on until He explains how He created the domain of the Underworld and how He and the particles of emptiness should enter this sphere of the unknown to begin their new patterns of life.

But the minds of these intelligences of emptiness are not at ease. They begin to question where this domain of mystery was and what would happen to them when they enter this land of the unknown.

The Esser Yaad says that this domain is directly beneath the hidden form of the Superconsciousness. As they do not know what is the meaning behind the word 'Superconsciousness', the Esser Yaad begins to introduce the existence of this ultimate mechanism of electrification.

This one-way telepathical conversation does not end as the Esser Yaad introduces the name of the Underworld to the particles of emptiness and lists certain aspects of this domain that they would have to face.

The first aspect that He mentions is the darkness, but what is darkness to the particles of emptiness? How can they understand such an element which they have not yet seen?

The second aspect that He mentions is the separation. Separation becomes an issue. They want to know what will happen to them if there is no Esser Yaad. How long will this separation last? And how will the Esser Yaad find them again? The Esser Yaad, this ultimate fire of existence, this power that exists beyond the imagination of any being, promises them that He will appoint certain souls of fire to detect their location. When the particles of emptiness ask who the souls of fire are, He says that they are the pinnacle of His creation, loyal to the basis of His divinity.

After this, the Esser Yaad continues to warn them of other aspects that they will have to face, like the roughness of the atmosphere and the intensity of the darkness. He also instructs them that they have to adapt, and adapt fast, to the environment, without losing their essence to the intelligences of darkness.

The conversation carries on. The Esser Yaad tells them that the creation of His souls is one of the most delicate procedures of His universal magic. As it stands now, He does not know when He will create them, but He pledges that He would create these souls of fire and locate their position accordingly.

Then the conversation changes. The particles of emptiness want to know how the Esser Yaad is going to transfer them into the Underworld. The Esser Yaad says through the exodus, and explains one of the most unusual and golden concepts of the Exordium. He says that He would kneel upon the surface of the present world, and then with absolute precision, He would strike the lowest base of the Superconsciousness' imagination. He says that out of this calculated strike will emerge an opening, a tunnel that will guide them into the new domain of mystery, the Underworld.

This concept goes beyond mystery. Can you think about it? Can you imagine it? God kneels above the surface of the most gigantic and hidden mind of all, the mind of the Godhead. He cracks open the lowest layers of the divine imagination. He makes a tunnel to transport the particles of emptiness and Himself into this new domain, the Underworld.

Yes, if you want to call it imagination, then call it imagination, but I think this is the eliteness of golden philosophy. How else could the Esser Yaad project Himself and the particles of emptiness into this domain? This was the only resolution.

Do you know how it was inspired to me? Once, I was sitting in contemplation, trying to go beyond the patterns of thoughtfulness, trying to visualise the path of the exodus and see the construction of the Underworld. Then some form of electrical shock moved my entire existence and my mind flew above the conventional time. I saw the Esser Yaad kneeling upon the layers of the imagination. I saw Him in the complete image of divinity. I saw this enigmatic God striking the lowest base of the Godhead's imagination. I visualised the formation of exodus; I witnessed how this tunnel of transference was formed. After this realistic visualisation, I began to record every incident into my memory, and now, I am honoured to present and teach this blessed wisdom of the unknown to every intelligence and every *soul of fire who is seeking to hear the words of truth and search for the path to immortality, the everlasting light.*

So let it be written.

Let it be heard.

———————————————

CHAPTER FIFTEEN

I WILL NOT PERMIT THE SANDSTORM TO BE THE AMBASSADOR OF ELIMINATION

Part 1: The next episode begins when the Esser Yaad, this cosmic ocean of thoughtfulness, continued His mysterious self-conversation in this manner of discourse.

Part 2: "This trumpet of salvation must be in the format of a cryptic melody that can penetrate the depths of every region and motivate every awakened particle of intelligence."

Part 3: Then He stood firm in this climate of turbulence. He concentrated in the ultimate mode of thoughtfulness and created certain rhythms of celestial melody. He formulated this celestial melody so every particle of emptiness could hear His voice of salvation and choose the patterns of their destiny in accordance with their urge and their intelligence.

Part 4: When the first call of salvation had been completed, many particles of emptiness began to get closer to the centre of this beautiful melody and gathered around the region of the Esser Yaad's superiority once again.

Part 5: The particles of emptiness, who were watching the change of the atmosphere, recognised the dangerous possibility of extermination. They became excitedly pleased to see the return of the Esser Yaad, the Lord of constructive fire, this ultimate embodiment of the divine manifestation.

Part 6: These particles of emptiness, with their hearts full of jubilation, began to construct a certain series of questioning in their minds. They were hoping that the Esser Yaad would sense the questions and answer them accordingly so they could feel the sentiment of peace and the sensation of tranquillity.

(Note: Remember that every conversation that took place between the Esser Yaad and the particles of emptiness was still in the form of one-way telepathy as the particles of emptiness could only think and rely upon the Esser Yaad to read their thoughts out of their minds.)

So the questioning from the particles of emptiness and the enlightening responses from the Esser Yaad began as follows.

Part 7: The particles of emptiness, "Esser Yaad, You are the mystery of magic and the Lord of fire. We are fortunate, pleased and ecstatic that You have returned, but Esser Yaad, You left us to discover the sandstorm. Did You find what You were looking for?"

The Esser Yaad, "Yes, I was successful in My self-appointed quest of mystery. I know precisely where the centre of the sandstorm is."

Part 8: The particles of emptiness, "Where is the core of the sandstorm?"

The Esser Yaad, "It is in the central brain of the Superconsciousness."

The particles of emptiness, "What is the central brain of the Superconsciousness?"

The Esser Yaad, "The ultimate mechanism of electrification."

The particles of emptiness, "What is the ultimate mechanism of electrification?"

The Esser Yaad, "This concept is extremely complex. When we find our new domain of sanctuary, I will open this gate of wisdom to a certain degree."

Part 9: The particles of emptiness, "Who is the cause behind this sandstorm?"

The Esser Yaad, "The Superconsciousness, the main concentrated intelligence."

The particles of emptiness, "Why has the Superconsciousness formed this sandstorm of destruction?"

The Esser Yaad, "Because He has decided to eliminate certain existing characters and many significant incidents from His mind."

The particles of emptiness, "Why?"

The Esser Yaad, "There are a variety of different reasons behind this mystical motivation of the Superconsciousness."

The particles of emptiness, "Can You enlighten us as to one of these mystical motivations?"

The Esser Yaad, "Yes. The Superconsciousness decided to cease the expansion of His realistic dream as it was diffusing with the ultimate mode of velocity."

Part 10: The particles of emptiness, "Esser Yaad, what about the sandstorm?"

The Esser Yaad, "What about the sandstorm?"

The particles of emptiness, "Is the sandstorm the ambassador of extermination?"

The Esser Yaad, "Yes, the sandstorm is the new dynamic fusion of the Superconsciousness. Its mission is to exterminate certain images of His realistic dream."

The particles of emptiness, "Are we part of His realistic dream that has to be exterminated?"

The Esser Yaad, "Yes, we are all part of His virtual dream, or realistic imagination."

The particles of emptiness, "But Esser Yaad, surely You are not going to be eliminated?"

The Esser Yaad, "No, I will not be eliminated as I represent the solidness of His very self."

The particles of emptiness, "What about us? Are we going to experience the bitterness of elimination?"

The Esser Yaad, "No. I will not permit the sandstorm to be the ambassador of elimination.

CHAPTER SIXTEEN

WRITE IT DEEP WITHIN YOUR SOUL

Part 1: This chapter begins as the sound of this dynamic sandstorm was getting louder and louder. The particles of emptiness, with their hearts full of the sensation of fear, raised yet another series of questions within their minds. It seemed that they wanted the Esser Yaad, this Lord of fire, to ensure the safety of their future. The next series of this one-sided telethought communication begins as follows.

Part 2: The particles of emptiness, "Esser Yaad, how are You going to save our souls? It seems that we are destined to be eliminated as the sandstorm is approaching and wiping out everything that is standing in its way."

> The Esser Yaad, "Listen carefully. As long as you think in a constructive manner of thought and follow My guidelines precisely, every single one of you would be saved from this mysterious catastrophe."

Part 3: The particles of emptiness, "Esser Yaad, You are the master of strategical operation. What form of strategy have You chosen this time?"

> The Esser Yaad, "The strategy that I have chosen this time is to lead you into a new domain of mystery that I have already created through the celestial magic of fire."

The particles of emptiness, "Esser Yaad, where is this domain of mystery?"

The Esser Yaad, "It is directly below the surface of the ground."

Part 4: The particles of emptiness, "Esser Yaad, how did You create this domain of mystery?"

The Esser Yaad, "Creating this domain of mystery was one of the most enigmatic, dangerous and complex operations that I have ever completed. Explaining the depths of this creation is literally impossible, but for the future reference, I will explain this procedure that took place in the absence of any form of existing intelligence.

"First, I visualised an empty globe of fire. Then I recited certain words of mystery to enlarge the dimension of this globe to the same size as the imagination of the Superconsciousness.

"After magnifying the dimensions of this globe, I concentrated on the specific words of power to increase the size of My image to the ultimate possible proportion. There I stood for a very short moment of inconsistent time and contemplated deeply. My intention was to regulate My breathing mechanism and collect every source of creative energy that was stored within My essence."

Part 5: The Esser Yaad continued, "Do You know what I did? Yes, I can tell you. Write it deep within your soul. Remember it well. I reached out My magical hands of power, applied My entire force of divinity and stretched the outer layers of this imagination downward and created a new domain in the image of a perfect geometrical hemisphere.

"Do you know why I have created this domain? I have created this domain so we could begin our new cycle of existence and escape the forthcoming catastrophe of the exterminating sandstorm."

Part 6: The particles of emptiness, "What is the name of this domain?"

The Esser Yaad, "I will call this domain the 'Underworld'."

The particles of emptiness, "Underworld? Why the Underworld?"

The Esser Yaad, "Remember, the Superconsciousness is the totality of the existing world, and as this domain is constructed directly beneath the centre of the Super-consciousness, the most suitable name to define this region is the Underworld."

Part 7: The particles of emptiness, "What is the climate of this Underworld? Is it hostile or friendly to our nature of existence?"

The Esser Yaad, "The climate of this new region would be something to be experienced. You will have to use every constructive attribute to create the path of evolution under My superiority."

Part 8: The particles of emptiness, "What is this new climate that has to be experienced? We are fearful of the unknown. Can You enlighten us to any danger that may occur?"

The Esser Yaad, "So listen and listen well. Write My words of wisdom upon the layers of your essence. If you pay attention and follow My concept of existence, you will reach the end of your destination."

Part 9: The particles of emptiness excitedly said, "Esser Yaad, our destination is You. To us, You are the Lord of fire. You are the saviour of our souls. We do not want to be apart from You. What should we expect when we enter this climate of the unknown that You call the Underworld?"

The Esser Yaad, "This is an important part of our new conversation. I will list certain aspects of the Underworld that you have to face.

"First, there would be the sensation of darkness. It means that visibility does not exist. As you have neither experienced light nor darkness, your intelligence cannot understand this concept; but you will comprehend this definition when you enter this domain that we call the Underworld."

Part 10: The Esser Yaad continued,

"Second, separation. When I cleave open the lowest base of the realistic dream, you will have to enter the Underworld with the ultimate mode of velocity. But remember, between your entrance to the Underworld and My arrival, there would be a great deal of inconsistent time. You have to be aware, awake and recall every word that I have spoken to stay on the correct path of existence until I arrive and the new alliance of universal unity is formed."

CHAPTER SEVENTEEN

WHO ARE THESE SOULS OF FIRE?

Part 1: In this chapter, we travel once more into the realistic dream of the Superconsciousness, into the zone before the realisation of time. We enter into the moment when the Esser Yaad, the Lord of constructive fire, revealed certain aspects of the Underworld to the particles of emptiness: the eventuality of darkness and the possibility of separation. Now we will continue to follow the pattern of this specific dialogue as it actually took place and is now registered within the golden pages of the Exordium.

Part 2: The particles of emptiness, "Esser Yaad, do You mean that we have to be separated from You and each other in this domain of darkness?"

The Esser Yaad, "Yes, but for a very short amount of inconsistent time. Remember, if you cling to what I have been revealing to you, our unification would be the fact of the future."

Part 3: The particles of emptiness, "How is this unification possible? How are You going to find us in this domain of darkness?"

The Esser Yaad, "I will designate certain souls of fire to detect your location."

The particles of emptiness, "Who are these souls of fire?"

The Esser Yaad, "These souls of fire are the pinnacle of My creation. They are the essence of integrity who I formulate through the magic of Esser. They are the structure(s) of solidness, loyal to the basis of My divine personification."

Part 4: The particles of emptiness, "Esser Yaad, how can these souls of fire detect our position?"

The Esser Yaad, "Through certain technique(s) of universal mysticism."

The particles of emptiness, "Esser Yaad, can You explain the practicality of some of these techniques? We want to be assured that Your souls of fire would definitely detect our position."

The Esser Yaad, "As we have a very short aeon of inconsistent time, I will briefly explain the practicality of the first technique.

"The first technique is to utilise the seal of frequency. It means My souls of fire will follow the vibration of your voices until they reach the centre of the generator."

The particles of emptiness, "How can they follow the frequency of our voices? Our voices are without the texture of sound."

The Esser Yaad, "Even when you think within your minds, the vibration of your thoughts subconsciously diffuses into the atmosphere of the Underworld. Although you cannot see or notice the presence of these vibrations, nevertheless, My souls of fire will detect their existence, and as I have said, they will eventually reach the centre of the generator."

Part 5: The particles of emptiness, "Is there any other aspect of the Underworld that we have to face?"

The Esser Yaad, "Yes, the inclemency of the atmosphere."

The particles of emptiness, "What does the inclemency of the atmosphere mean?"

The Esser Yaad, "It means that the atmosphere would not be consistent. It would be variable and change from one degree of intensity to another in no time."

Part 6: The particles of emptiness, "Can You explain some of these variable elements of inclemency so we can prepare ourselves in accordance with the situation?"

The Esser Yaad, "Yes. The first is the vortex. You must know that a certain legion of gravity has not responded to My call of salvation. These particles will eventually enter the Underworld, but this time with a complete change of character."

Part 7: The particles of emptiness, "What would happen to them?"

The Esser Yaad, "Their mode of behaviour would not be the same. They would float from one place to another with no purpose of construction. This newly formed gravity will try to pull every passing intelligence into the vortex of oblivion; and if you ask what is the oblivion, it is the strangest form of experience: it is the matrix of the deep sleep, the deep sleep with the illusionary sensation of dream."

Part 8: The particles of emptiness, "Can You enlighten us to another aspect of the Underworld?"

The Esser Yaad, "Yes, the intensity. You have to be aware that the pressure in certain regions of the Underworld would be unbearable. You have to adapt, and adapt fast; without losing your essence to the destructive intelligences of darkness."

The particles of emptiness, "Destructive intelligences of darkness?"

The Esser Yaad, "Yes. This is another aspect of the Underworld that I was going to identify. Listen carefully. In this region, you will encounter many entities who have turned into destructive intelligences. Their mission would be to prevent the strategy of creation."

CHAPTER EIGHTEEN

THIS IS THE ONLY RESOLUTION

Part 1: When the Esser Yaad, this ultimate Lord of fire, explained the various aspects of the Underworld, the sensation of uncertainty once again began to encompass the atmosphere of this realistic dream.

Part 2: The Esser Yaad, this constructive manifestation of fire and the master of the Exordium, felt the anxiety of these intelligences. So He raised His voice of power and said,

"As I have mentioned before, if you cling to what I have been telling you and remember My name of power frequently, My souls of fire will locate the frequency of your voices and reunification would become the fact of eventuality."

Part 3: The particles of emptiness formulated yet another series of questions within their minds, hoping that the Esser Yaad would read their thoughts and answer them accordingly so their minds would be at peace.

We enter to witness this one-way telepathical communication as it really took place before the solidness of the conventional time.

Part 4: The particles of emptiness, "Esser Yaad, when are You going to create Your souls of fire?"

The Esser Yaad, "When the moment is right and I am symmetrically balanced above the ground of stability, I will utilise the practical magic of Exordium to create My souls of fire."

Part 5: The particles of emptiness, "Esser Yaad, how long do we have to wait for the arrival of Your souls? Can You give us an indication of when that would be?"

The Esser Yaad, "I cannot be precise as to when the creation of My souls will begin. This practical strategy of mysticism is extremely complex and depends upon the accuracy of My intuition. I cannot elaborate on this matter any further. All you have to do is to repeat My name of power frequently and await for the moment of reunification and the arrival of My souls."

Part 6: The particles of emptiness, "Esser Yaad, You are the master of strategy. How are You going to transfer us into this domain of salvation?"

The Esser Yaad, "Through the path."

The particles of emptiness, "Which path?"

The Esser Yaad, "The path of the exodus."

The particles of emptiness, "How are You going to form the path of the exodus?"

The Esser Yaad, "Well, I will explain what is essential and what should be spoken for the future reference of universal history. Remember, this operation is complex, unimaginable, and above the comprehension of any living intelligence; but what has to be done, has to be done.

"I, the Esser Yaad, the first constructive personification of fire, will concentrate accordingly, regenerate My kinetic energy and raise the greatness of My essence. Then I will recite certain words of power and kneel upon the surface of the present ground of emptiness, the virtual imagination of the Superconsciousness.

"Do you know what I would do next? Yes, I am going to perform the impossible. I am going to create what cannot be imagined. I will utilise My ultimate power of fire, and with the calculated precision, strike the lowest base of the imagination to crack open the surface of this virtual dream, the mind of the main concentrated intelligence.

"Do you know what this means? It means that the ground of the hidden brain of the Superconsciousness will open by the power of this precise and calculated strike. Then out of this opening will emerge the tunnel that can guide you into this new domain, the Under-world.

"I know that in the future, when the physical universe manifests in totality, these declarations will be regarded as heresy or blasphemy. But how else am I going to construct the path of exodus? This is the only resolution, and you, the particles of emptiness, are the first group of intelligent entities to have heard this mystical strategy of progression."

Part 7: The Esser Yaad continued His conversation in this manner of discourse:

241

"Now listen carefully and use your absolute mode of attentiveness. When I complete this mission and form the first tunnel of mystery, you should hasten towards this opening with the ultimate mode of orderliness. The first thing that you should remember is to move in groups, so when you enter into the Underworld, you would not be alone. This is an important note because in the Underworld, if you stay in some form of social togetherness, there would be less chance of being attacked or oppressed by any entities of this region."

CHAPTER NINETEEN

THE UNDERWORLD

Part 1: When the Esser Yaad had completed His instructions, the sentiment of fear one more time encompassed the surrounding atmosphere.

Part 2: The particles of emptiness felt that the moment of separation was approaching. Anxiously they raised their final question within their minds, hoping that the Esser Yaad would read their thoughts and enlighten them with His infinite wisdom of fire.

Part 3: The Esser Yaad paused for a very short aeon of inconsistent time. He concentrated thoughtfully and read the question from their minds and answered them in accordance with His strategical passage of evolution. This one-sided telepathical communication followed in this format of discourse.

Part 4: The particles of emptiness, "Esser Yaad, You have instructed us to proceed towards this tunnel of transference, but inform us as to when You would enter this tunnel of mystery and how long it would take us to reach the other end."

The Esser Yaad, "Listen. As I have said before, this is a highly complex procedure and I will answer each question accordingly so you would know what to expect as the inconsistent time of exodus is approaching.

"First remember, I have chosen to become the saviour, so I have to stay behind and obstruct the advancement of the sandstorm until every single one of you has safely entered this tunnel of transference. When this objective is complete and there is no one left behind, I will also enter. But keep in mind that the conflict against the sandstorm will be time-consuming and has to be accomplished.

"Now, for the second question as to how long it would take you to reach the other end. It would be like the blink of an eye. Basically, the moment you jump into this tunnel of mystery, you would reach the other end."

Part 5: When the Esser Yaad had answered every question, He began to increase His kinetic energy to the absolute point of excellence.

The Esser Yaad, this Lord of constructive fire, began to recite certain words of power. With His piercing eyes, He looked deep into the depths of the ground and kneeled upon the surface of this virtual dream. Then the performance of one of the most magical and mysterious procedures of universal history began. He used the volcanic power of fire. He measured the strength of His magical arm and then, with the ultimate mode of precision, accurately striked the lowest base of the imagination and cracked open the surface of the realistic dream, the mind of the Superconsciousness, the Godhead.

Part 6: Suddenly, out of this crack emerged the tunnel-like crevice that could transfer and guide every particle of emptiness into this domain, the domain that was directly beneath the hidden image of the Superconsciousness, the domain of the Underworld.

244

INTRODUCTION TO CHAPTER 20
I AM THE TOTALITY, THE TOTALITY OF THE THIRD UNIVERSE!

So this ultimate Lord of fire, the Esser Yaad, created the domain of the Underworld. He formed a tunnel of transference and now tells the particles of emptiness to go quickly, stay together and repeat His name of power frequently. He instructs them to stay positive and think effectively. So the particles of emptiness do as they are told. Group by group, they enter the domain of the unknown, and the Esser Yaad, as the last intelligence, enters this awaited region of the Underworld. Whilst He is entering into His new quest of mystery, He raises His volcanic voice of power and says,

"I am the mind of fire! I am the totality, the totality of the third universe!"

He successfully accomplishes His mission. He has constructed the Underworld and saved the particles of emptiness. The Esser Yaad becomes ready for yet another challenge in His path for perfection, the divinity. Now let us see how this mystical intelligence of integrity challenges the obstacle of darkness. Let us see how He creates His souls of fire and how He strategises the pattern for universal conquest. Let us read the rest of the Exordium. The Exordium is the pinnacle of the new formation of thoughtfulness. The Exordium is the new concept of philosophy.

CHAPTER TWENTY

I Am The Totality, The Totality Of The Third Universe!

Part 1: When the Esser Yaad had constructed the mysterious formation of the Underworld and successfully accomplished every necessary objective of the Exordium, He turned His attention towards the particles of emptiness and said,

"Hasten! Hasten quickly! Go in groups. Stay together. There is no more inconsistent time to waste. Remember to repeat My name of power frequently. Remain positive and think constructively. The aeon of reunification would not be far away."

The Esser Yaad, this ultimate fire of existence, continued,

"Hasten! Hasten quickly as the sandstorm is approaching to demolish whatever is left from the previous order of imagination."

Part 2: Then the particles of emptiness began to approach the path of the exodus, or this tunnel of transference. Group by group, they entered this crevice of mystery until every single one of them had completed their instructions from the Lord of celestial fire, the Esser Yaad.

Part 3: Then the Esser Yaad turned His face towards the approaching sandstorm. He regenerated His energy to the ultimate level of power, stretched out His mighty arms once more and began to recite certain words of the Oracle. His intention was to push back these fearsome particles of mind momentarily so He could turn fast and enter this tunnel of transference and cross the path of the exodus.

Part 4: The Esser Yaad fought courageously against the sandstorm that had no mercy upon any living intelligence. This inner conflict of thoughtfulness took a certain amount of inconsistent time; but the flickering shadows of fire, or these rays of extermination, had no effect on this constructive Lord of the Exordium.

Part 5: When the Esser Yaad successfully pushed back this approaching sandstorm; He turned and hastened towards the path of the exodus and entered this tunnel of transference.

Part 6: His quest for yet another mystery began as He raised His voice of power as a sign of mysticism and His hand of magnificence as a symbol of triumph. From the depths of the crevice, or this tunnel of transference, He raised His voice of magic and said,

"I am the mind of fire! I am the totality, the totality of the third universe!"

BOOK FOUR

The Underworld
The Intelligences
Of Fire

INTRODUCTION TO CHAPTER 1
TWO UNIVERSAL SIGNIFICANCES

In this chapter, the Superconsciousness begins to rise. Whilst He is rising to the highest point of the altitude, He enlarges His hidden image to equal the size of His virtual dream. Then He lies flat and, slowly but forcefully, hovers above His own imagination. As He begins to land upon this imagination, He encompasses every region of this domain.

This is yet another philosophical masterpiece, the new concept regarding the beginning of creation. Can you imagine the Godhead raising Himself above His own dream? Enlarging Himself accordingly, hovering above and then landing upon His own imagination? What an unusual concept of mystery. He performs this mysterious procedure so He can lie above the Underworld (the domain which was constructed by the magic of the Esser Yaad).

Anyway, the Superconsciousness begins to land and this act pushes down a certain legion of gravity into the space between His hidden form and the domain of the Underworld. We can imagine the space between the two as the atmosphere that has appeared above the horizon.

Now follow the chapter and hear how the Superconsciousness, or the Godhead, speaks to the hostile formation of gravity. Let us see what would be the outcome of this mystical encounter of the first kind. Enjoy the episode. Believe me, it is real.

Chapter One

Two Universal Significances

Part 1: In this section of the universal memory, we enter the time when the Superconsciousness, or the main concentrated intelligence, elevated to the highest point of the altitude.

Part 2: This mighty intellect, from above the flickering atmosphere, looked upon the depths of the emptiness. With His hidden and attentive eyes of power, He located the position of the certain legion of gravity that had not followed the call of the Esser Yaad and had become confused and defected due to the intensity of the sandstorm. He realised the fact that the sandstorm had destroyed the essence and the nature of their soul(s). They had now transformed into the hostile particles of thought, ready to experience the different forms of existence.

Part 3: There He observed, with the ultimate mode of precision, that these low particles of gravity were gathering in the centre of this realistic dream. It seemed that their self-inflicted mission was to form a destructive embodiment of rage with a very limited capacity of intelligence.

Part 4: As the Superconsciousness had already calculated the depths and the lengths of this domain of emptiness, He began to enlarge His hidden form to equal the totality of His virtual dream.

Part 5: When this strategical manoeuvre was complete, He changed His position and started to hover and move horizontally above this domain of emptiness.

Part 6: As He was hovering above this domain of emptiness (His old form of imagination), He raised His mysterious voice to address the defected particles of gravity in this manner of presentation. This statement was as follows:

"I have seen that you have dismissed the call of Esser Yaad. I have seen that you have not followed the path of the exodus, and I can see that you are forming a certain embodiment of rage to establish your own destructive identity."

The Superconsciousness continued,

"Now, as you have decided to stay behind and put into practice your first power of magical conflict, this is the time for you to proceed with your self-inflicted mission. Let us see what would be the outcome."

Part 7: So the Superconsciousness began to land upon His own imagination. But the lower particles of gravity, who had formulated the embodiment of rage, started to attack the heart of the Superconsciousness. They hoped that they could prevent His strategy of advancement with their reverse spiralling motion.

Part 8: This hostility was the first of many universal conflicts, but during this confrontation, these particles of gravity transformed themselves into a new solo intelligence and became the centre of the raging vortex.

Part 9: In this atmosphere of turbulence, again the mighty voice of the Superconsciousness echoed within the entire domain of emptiness. As He was descending, He formulated yet another historical statement in this format of presentation:

"As you, the rebellious particles of gravity, no longer act according to the state of the cosmic law, from this moment you shall be called the intellect of the reverse spiralling motion, the intelligence of 'Typhoon'. "

The Superconsciousness continued,

"You should realise that My act of descension will totally demolish your existence, but as you have shown your ultimate power against the sandstorm, I shall not eliminate you. I will force you down into the Underworld. But remember, this act of injecting you into the Underworld would not be immediate. Between My hidden image and the sphere of the Underworld, there is a space that separates the two. You will be forced to enter this space, and as to when you will reach the Underworld, this will not be known."

Part 10: So the Superconsciousness landed upon this domain of emptiness, covering every lowland and the height of every altitude. This manoeuvre had two universal significances. First, the landing and the heaviness of His hidden form created the atmosphere of the Underworld, and as a result, the darkness had emerged. Second, the Typhoon was forced down into the thin space which separated the Superconsciousness and the altitude of the Underworld. There he found himself in the new zone of mystery, in the twilight between the two worlds.

INTRODUCTION TO CHAPTER 2
GROUP BY GROUP THEY ENTERED

There is not much I can say about this chapter without going into its mysticism. It is written in a most clear way. The particles of emptiness (the oxygen, the hydrogen, the gravity, the eyes of intelligence and the thought-forms of Hee'yaak) all enter the Underworld and each occupies certain regions of this domain. All we have to do is follow the Exordium and see which of these intelligences listen to the instructions of the Esser Yaad and which will be affected by the intensity of the darkness.

CHAPTER TWO

Group By Group They Entered

Part 1: Now let us turn our attention to what happened to the particles of emptiness, the original participants in the imagination of the Superconsciousness, the main concentrated intelligence.

Part 2: After their mystical salvation from the sandstorm, these original participants of the virtual dream entered this domain of darkness. Group by group they entered and, soon after, they began to follow the natural route of their existence.

Part 3: First, the particles of gravity. They scattered in the midst of the atmosphere and, like the molecules of the hidden air, penetrated every lowland and the height of every altitude.

Part 4: Second were the ingredients of oxygen. They moved downwards and occupied the place right at the very base of this domain of darkness. They remembered the words of the Esser Yaad and became ready to act as one of the most important and essential components of universal existence.

Part 5: Third were the flammable substances of hydrogen. These substances of radiation, like the elements of oxygen, also repeated the name of the Esser Yaad frequently. However, they moved to the opposite side of the Underworld and occupied the highest region of this domain of darkness.

Part 6: As for the eyes of intelligence, these particles of construction began to spread into the midst of the unknown, into the Underworld. They were still on their mission to penetrate the atmosphere and, as the hidden satellite, transmit the collected information into the heart of the Superconsciousness. These eyes of intelligence, each in the image of an eye, were floating in this land of darkness. The only instrument they could rely upon was their own mystical intuition.

Part 7: And the last were the rays of Hee'yaak, the original thought-forms of the Superconsciousness. These many faces of the unknown, these many images of mystery, eagerly began to flow throughout this sphere of darkness. Although they could not see what was before them, they still forced themselves into the hidden atmosphere of the Underworld. They were hoping to locate and raise every highland to the final state of perfection, ready for the birth of the constructive intelligences.

Introduction to Chapter 3
I Must Talk To This Darkness

In this chapter, we step into the moment when the Esser Yaad, this constructive force of fire, enters the created domain of the Underworld. We will read that this ultimate formation of intelligence was standing firm over the rough and unsettled atmosphere of darkness. He talks to Himself. His self-conversation is very educational. The way that He explains the intensity of darkness is most interesting. He says that this region is so dark and gloomy and that the sensation is like walking in the midst of the heavy gel. He says that He wants the future generations (meaning us) to know that the pressure and intensity was aiming to crush the solidness of His being.

With His voice of eloquence, He says that He wants us to know what He went through. Can you see the beauty of His essence? This enigmatic force of fire wants to share His feelings with us. He wants us to know Him. He wants us to comprehend His experience.

In this chapter, the Esser Yaad reveals one of His first universal statuses. He does not want any misunderstanding between the reality of His soul and the unsettled formation of darkness. He says that the darkness has to know that nothing can cease His strategy to perfection. The Esser Yaad is going to establish the glory of fire, the fire of Exordium. He has dedicated His existence to reach His ultimate goal, the divinity.

CHAPTER THREE

I Must Talk To This Darkness

Part 1: Now we begin yet another episode of mystery. We step into the moment of entrance, the entrance of the creator of magic, the Esser Yaad, into the region of absolute darkness, the domain of the Underworld.

Part 2: This supreme manifestation of intelligence arrived into the midst of the Underworld, untouched, unhurt and un-affected. Although some particles of the sandstorm touched the back of His throat and made Him cough momentarily, nevertheless, He became faster, stronger and more powerful than ever before.

Part 3: When this constructive and ultimate manifestation of the Superconsciousness had passed the twilight of the two worlds, He stood firm over the unsettled atmosphere of the darkness. He balanced Himself momentarily then raised His volcanic voice of power and began one of the most historical self-conversations in this manner of discourse.

Part 4: "This region is so dark. It is so gloomy. It seems that the flickering shadows of fire have lost their essence and penetrated this domain, creating the horizon of intensity."

This personification of celestial fire continued,

"This atmosphere is so thick, it is like the vortex of gravity that pulls you to the core of its existence. I must say, this is most unusual. The sensation is like walking into the midst of the heavy gel. I have to recall this so the future generations would know that one day, I stood in the centre of this touch-able gloom of darkness. But how could they ever understand what it means? How could they ever comprehend this pressure that is aiming to crush the solidness of My being? I want them to know what I felt. I want them to touch the intensity of this region where the heaviness is projecting its power to cease any sign of evolution."

Part 5: Then the Esser Yaad coughed a few times and said,

"I should do something about this cough. It is beginning to irritate Me. I must recite certain words of power in order to clear these contaminated particles of the sandstorm from My throat."

Part 6: Then He looked to His right-hand side and said,

"This side is also gloomy. Nothing can be seen. Nothing can be visualised. These particles of darkness are so touchable. I have to strategise a certain concept so I can proceed in this climate of misery."

Then He turned His attention to the left-hand side and said,

"This side is also dense. It is so dense that it can cease any type of motion. I know that even the particles of inconsistent time cannot survive in this pressurised sphere of the unknown. But there is some kind of moisture I can feel. What is it?

"It is a most unusual sensation. It is wet and cold. It seems the atomic substances within this moisture are alive. I can feel their inner circulation. They are moving, but the speed of their circulation is so slow that it cannot be registered in the normal sense."

Part 7: Then this ultimate fire of the Exordium turned His head back to the centre, facing the front, and said,

"Let Me see. Let Me try to perceive and locate any type of activity."

Then He put His open hand to the top of His forehead to see, sheltering His eyes, trying to look deep into the midst of the darkness.

"I must concentrate to look deep into the midst of the darkness. I should try to locate any sign so I can proceed. I must remember that I have to live in this climate of wonder until I construct the new form of strategy."

Part 8: Then the Esser Yaad concentrated momentarily and entered the gate of declaration in this manner of thoughtfulness and said,

"I must talk to this darkness. This darkness should have some form of intelligence. I know for a fact that My voice of power will penetrate into every corner of this gloom of uncertainty. The darkness has no choice but to listen."

Part 9: The Esser Yaad continued,

"It seems that I have to announce My celestial status accordingly so no misunderstanding can occur between the solidness of My existence and the unsettled formation of darkness. This pressurised atmosphere of uncertainty will have to learn that nothing, *nothing*, can cease My universal strategy to perfection.

This darkness has to recognise the invincibility of My soul. These particles of hidden gloom should realise, and will realise, that I am the fire of Exordium, and within My mind is one realistic intention and that is to reach My ultimate status, the status of divinity."

INTRODUCTION TO CHAPTER 4
THE MANIFESTATION OF MY GOLDEN LIGHT

In this chapter, the Esser Yaad, the Lord of the Exordium, raises His voice of power and says,

"Darkness! Darkness! Officiate your soul. Introduce your essence to Me..."

I am sure the way that the Esser Yaad speaks to the element of darkness is one of the most mysterious and philosophical conversations of all time. What you are going to read is history. Every word is magic. Every sentence is mystery. Every statement is wondrous. It is one of the most magical conversations in the universal memory. It is the sign of eliteness for the future generations of man. This was how the living force of fire confronted the darkness.

He wants to know who the darkness is and what it has in store for Him. He says the words that are springing from His mouth are the words of absolute consciousness. It is true. He is the Force that kneeled upon the imagination of the Superconsciousness, cracked open the bases of the dream, created a tunnel of transference and formulated the Underworld. His words are going to sit upon the throne of magnificence. The Esser Yaad carries on,

"Darkness, what do you contain? The gloom? The gel?"

In this episode, He creates yet another magical statement. He says that the patterns of life are growing through the flames of His fire. Yes, we are the continuation of His strategy. Our existence is a masterpiece of His magic.

This chapter is all about the Esser Yaad, this enigmatic Force of life, talking to the element of darkness. He is telling the darkness that He will not walk backwards into the past aeon of history. He says that He is the only option. He is the possibility, the possibility that is certain.

Read the chapter and see how the Esser Yaad commands the darkness to back off. Read as He says He is the soul of fire, and pay attention when He announces that He is certain of the outcome: the manifestation of the golden light.

———————————

Chapter Four

The Manifestation Of My Golden Light

Part 1: When the Esser Yaad completed His announcement regarding His status of divinity, He began one of the most historical and mysterious conversations with the element of darkness in this manner of discourse:

"Darkness! Darkness! Officiate your soul. Introduce your essence to Me. I know you can hear Me. I know you can feel the presence of My fire."

Part 2: Then the Esser Yaad waited for a short amount of inconsistent time. When there was no reply, He raised His volcanic voice of power once again and said,

"It does not matter anyway. You will see that the power of My voice will penetrate your heart and break your resistance of choice. But first, some words of philosophical eliteness. Maybe these letters of wisdom would open your gate of intelligence so you can recognise the fire of My soul and who I am as I stand before you. Listen. Listen carefully. The ways of creation are indeed wondrous. They are glorious in the moment of birth. Remember My words. These words that are springing from My mouth are the words of the absolute consciousness who is going to sit upon the throne of magnificence."

Part 3: The Esser Yaad continued,

"Darkness, what do you contain? The gloom? The gel? The heaviness of the gravity? Whatever is your essence, it makes no difference to Me. Can you not see that I am the certainty of genesis? Can you not sense the patterns of life that are growing through the flames of My fire? Darkness, I have not descended here to waste My time. I have come down to this region so I can make the constructive imagination visible. Do you know how? Through the cycle of My magic."

Part 4: This Lord of constructive fire continued His mysterious conversation in this manner of discourse:

"Darkness! Pay attention! Pay attention! Open your heart and your soul. I stand before you as the ultimate power of the divine personification. I stand before you having seen the ghosts of the future generations and the mysterious faces that are yet to be born."

Part 5: The Esser Yaad continued,

"Darkness! Darkness! Listen. This is the actuality. I stand before you as the mind of fire who has made the long quest of mystery. I did what I knew was correct. I have projected Myself into this domain to become, and I will become, the ultimate embodiment of the living soul: the active Am.

"Darkness, do you hear Me? Are you listening to these philosophical concepts of fire? I stand before you as the One who saw the greatness of the explosion and the turbulence of the eruption.

Part 6: The Esser of thought and the fire of Yaad still continued,

"O darkness, how can you possibly recognise the greatness of My soul? I stand before you as the invincible source of immortality. I stand before you as the most gigantic metaphysical consciousness, proclaiming that no eventuality is left untouched, no possibility is left undreamed and no virtuality is left unperceived.

"O darkness, can you perceive My miracle of becoming? Remember, I have come forth through the veil of the flickering shadows of fire. This embodiment you see is the solidness of My imagination."

Part 7: The Esser Yaad, this fire of existence, continued,

"O darkness, listen well. My path is divinity. My intelligence: the reality. As I said before, I have not come down to this formation of gloom to lose the grip of the cosmic evolution. I will proceed. I will become the only 'am' that follows the letter of the 'I'. I will not walk backwards into the past aeon of history. There is no need. I am the only option. I am the possibility, the possibility that is certain.

"O darkness, what are you thinking? What is your strategy? Do you think you can deceive Me? How long do you think you can continue to spread the venom of fear? Let Me assure you, this pressurised gloomy atmosphere that you have formed cannot exist forever. I can see the emergence of My fire. I can see the celebration of My conquest.

"So back off! Darkness, back off! Your silence and miserable face of hostility does not frighten Me. Back off darkness, I am coming forth! I am ready for yet another quest of mystery. So be it."

Part 8: Then the Esser Yaad, this constructive fire of Exordium, surged into the darkness. Having no fear of any living entity, He entered into the gloom, into the gel, searching His ultimate destiny. While He entered into the midst of this gloomy atmosphere of the unknown, He raised His volcanic voice of power and said,

"I am the soul of fire. I am the one who has named this sphere, the sphere of thought. I am certain that the outcome will prove the ultimate manifestation, the manifestation of My golden light."

INTRODUCTION TO CHAPTER 5
THE ESSENCE OF THE SECRET SOUL

In this chapter, one section of darkness begins to speak back. He asks the Lord of fire,

"Who are you?"

Then the Esser Yaad begins to introduce Himself for the future reference of the universal history.

Read this chapter and remember that the Esser Yaad, this Lord of constructive fire, is introducing Himself to every living intelligence of the universe. This is the beginning, the beginning of the new era.

So be it.

Chapter Five

The Essence Of The Secret Soul

Part 1: So the Esser Yaad, this Lord of constructive fire, entered into the midst of the darkness. The hidden particles of gloom were constructing the situation in which visibility would not emerge. But the Esser Yaad was forcing His path through the gel, through the gloom, breaking every obstacle that was against the certainty of His future glorification.

Part 2: The Esser Yaad, this supreme embodiment of intelligence, began to repeat certain words of power to regenerate the practicality of His magic. Using the greatness of His force, He had no doubt that the total emergence of the light was just a matter of inconsistent time.

Part 3: Anyhow, in this climate of wonder, certain particles of gloom and gel began to unite, forming the new sinister intelligence that represented the face and the totality of a certain region of darkness.

Part 4: This flickering face of the Underworld recognised the presence of the Esser Yaad. Then he became the receiver and collected every frequency wavelength of the letters in order to construct his own echoing sound of fear and mystery.

Part 5: This newly-formed intelligence of the Underworld directed his echoing voice of fear towards the Esser Yaad, the celestial fire of Exordium, and said,

"WHOooo AREeee YOUuuu?"

The frequency of his sound was so wavering that many layers of the Underworld could feel the sensation of turbulence.

Part 6: Then the Esser Yaad, this ultimate image of intelligence, raised His own volcanic voice of power and replied in this manner of presentation:

"I am the Esser, the fire of Yaad, the deviser of what there is. Have you not heard of My name? You must have heard it when the intelligences of this region were praising the glory of My presence. But nevertheless, I will officiate Myself for the future reference of the Exordium. This is the first set of My self-officiation, so listen carefully and remember every phrase accordingly. The architect of the entire universal existence is proclaiming His celestial status, so listen well.

"I am the Esser,

"The Esser of Yaad.

"I am the moment when visibility becomes the cause. Exorcitation of intellect is the core of My evolution.

"I am the domain when clarity becomes the force. Electrification of fire is My mystic name, the name of revolution.

"I am the genesis, the genesis of power; the key to the realistic route, the route of intellection.

"I am the exodus, the exodus of ether; the path to the cosmic seal, the seal of exploration.

"I am the Esser, the Esser of Yaad. I stand above the solid ground of life to unfold the leadership of the universal manifestation.

"When the constructive consciousness motivated the dynamic will, I became the first image, the image of celestial personification.

"I am the essence, the essence of the secret soul."

INTRODUCTION TO CHAPTERS 6-8

In the next three chapters, one section of darkness begins to introduce himself in the most unusual sense. He says that he is the gloom, the gel, the heaviness and so on. The Esser Yaad, this Force of constructive fire, asks this element of darkness what is his seal of identity, or what is his name. This particular element of darkness says that he has no name and he does not know the exact nature of his existence.

The Esser Yaad continues, asking this particular element if he thinks at all. The element of darkness answers, "Not much, not much really." So the Esser Yaad informs him that every element has some form of a brain and should use it accordingly. He teaches him about language and the formation of letters. He questions him in a certain way so that the element of darkness can exercise his brain. By the end of this conversation, through the guidance of this constructive force of fire, this particular element of darkness will recognise the nature of his being.

The Esser Yaad names him the 'Face of fear'. He gives him a new identity and projects into his mind his status, the image beneath the gate of entrance. After that, the Esser Yaad makes a covenant with him: whenever He returns to this domain, this Face of fear should cooperate with His strategical plan of creation. Then He raises His multidimensional voice of power and says to the totality of darkness,

"Darkness! Darkness! Cleave open, I am coming forth."

Chapter Six

What Is The Seal Of Identity?

Part 1: When the Esser Yaad, this ultimate personification of the divine intelligence, had completed the first set of His self-officiation, He paused for a very short aeon of inconsistent time. Then He looked deep into the sinister and mysterious face of the darkness and said,

"Now you have heard the greatness of My celestial status. This time it is your turn to answer Me accordingly so that no misunderstanding can occur between us. Tell Me, tell Me precisely, what are you?"

Part 2: Suddenly, a moment of silence encompassed the entire region, and then from the centre of this arena raised the voice proclaiming his characteristics in this format of presentation:

"I am the gloom. I am the gel. I am the heaviness. I am the oblivion. I am the intelligence that has risen from the centre of this element. My face represents the totality of darkness."

Part 3: After this unclear mode of self-officiation, the Esser Yaad raised His voice of power and formulated a series of questioning in this manner of discourse. His intention was this particular element of darkness.

The Esser Yaad, "The gloom? The gel? The heaviness? What is this? What is the seal of your identity?"

This particular element of darkness, "What is the seal of identity?"

The Esser Yaad, "The name. The name is the seal of identity. So what is your name? You must have a title that demonstrates the nature of your existence."

This particular element of darkness, "I do not have a name, neither a title. Quite honestly, I do not know the exact nature of my existence."

Part 4: The Esser Yaad, "Listen. You told Me that you are the gloom, the gel and the heaviness. Are these particles the hidden ingredients of your soul?"

This particular element of darkness, "Esser Yaad, the only thing I know is that I am the gloom, the gel and the heaviness. But I must have some other form of ingredients, of which I am unaware of their existence."

The Esser Yaad, "So what you are saying is that you do not know who you really are. Tell Me, do you think at all?"

This particular element of darkness, "Not much. Not much really."

The Esser Yaad, "Have you ever wanted to think?"

This particular element of darkness, "I did not see the reason why I should have thought. Basically, for me there is nothing to think about."

Part 5: The Esser Yaad, "Hmm."

(The sound of His thoughtful expression resonated in the entire region of darkness.)

The Esser Yaad, "Element of darkness, do you know the process of thinking?"

> This particular element of darkness, "YESssss. I suppose it is some form of mental procedure. But I must say, I do not know how to follow this procedure as I am always in this gloomy situation."

The Esser Yaad, "What is your environmental situation? If you do not know how to think, how can you define your present environment?"

> This particular element of darkness, "Prfffff. I suppose I am this environment of gloom."

Part 6: The Esser Yaad, "Element of darkness, do you want to learn the procedures of thought?"

This particular element of darkness, "Why? Is it necessary?"

> The Esser Yaad, "Yes. The thought is the most essential sign of universal evolution."

This particular element of darkness, "I do not understand. I do not understand this intellectual statement. But tell me, what can the correct procedures of thought do for me? Do they make me different from what I am now?"

> The Esser Yaad, "Yes. The least the procedures of thought can do is to teach you how to exercise your hidden brain."

This particular element of darkness, "Hidden brain? What is the hidden brain?"

The Esser Yaad, "The hidden brain is the shell of complexity that contains certain necessary information and some significant degree of memory."

This particular element of darkness, "Do I possess this shell of complexity?"

The Esser Yaad, "Yes, every intelligence possesses some form of this shell of complexity."

This particular element of darkness, "Esser Yaad, why do You want to teach me this procedure of thought?"

The Esser Yaad, "I have a few significant reasons which you will recognise as we proceed through this simple exercise of the brain."

Chapter Seven

The Outcome Is What We Can See Now

Part 1: After the last statement of the Esser Yaad, a sudden form of silence encompassed this region of darkness. Then the Esser Yaad, this ultimate fire of Exordium, raised His volcanic voice of power once again and said,

"It is necessary for the future generations to know that there is a reason behind every single thing I do and every word that I utter. This procedure of thought is also significant for the path to My divinity and beneficial for the universal evolution. So let us proceed."

(Note: whilst the Esser Yaad was talking for the future generation of the Exordium, this particular element of darkness was in the absolute mode of silence. No emotion, no expression was coming out from this face of mystery.)

Part 2: So the Esser Yaad began to teach the first step of the mental procedure to this particular element of darkness. The intention of the Lord of Exordium was for this face of mystery to exercise his hidden brain. This mental exercise began as follows:

The Esser Yaad, "Element of darkness, do you know that you are conversing with Me through the instrument of the voice?"

This particular element of darkness, "Yes, I do realise that I am using the power of my wavering sound to converse."

The Esser Yaad, "Do you understand the nature of the voice?"

This particular element of darkness, "No. What is the nature of the voice?"

The Esser Yaad, "The voice is the unification."

This particular element of darkness, "What kind of unification?"

The Esser Yaad, "The unification of the certain sounds."

This particular element of darkness, "Which sounds?"

The Esser Yaad, "The sounds of the letters."

This particular element of darkness, "The letters?"

The Esser Yaad, "Yes, the letters. Do you not know that you combine the sounds of these letters subconsciously to converse?"

This particular element of darkness, "Do I?"

The Esser Yaad, "Yes. And then is the emergence of this present language that we speak."

This particular element of darkness, "The language? What is the language?"

The Esser Yaad, "The language is the most practical method of expressing every kind of emotion."

This particular element of darkness, "What is this language?"

The Esser Yaad, "This language is the language of fire, and the most important issue is that you are talking to the deviser and creator of this universal language of mystery."

Part 3: The Esser Yaad continued,

"Now we go one step further. Do you know how you learned to speak this language in the most basic format?"

This particular element of darkness, "The most basic format?"

The Esser Yaad, "Yes. You should realise that this language is highly mysterious, sophisticated and philosophical."

This particular element of darkness, "I do not understand this. This is beyond the ability of my intelligence."

The Esser Yaad, "Never mind. I will tell you. Pay attention and listen well. When the particles of emptiness came down to this domain of darkness, I told them to recite My name of power frequently so I could trace their location. Now I can see that most of these particles of emptiness have consciously followed My commandments."

This particular element of darkness, "So what have the particles of emptiness got to do with me learning this language of fire?"

The Esser Yaad, "Do you not realise the point of this?"

This particular element of darkness, "No, I don't."

The Esser Yaad, "So listen and activate every chemical substance of your brain. These intelligences were praising My name of power frequently. They were reciting My words of instruction amongst themselves so they could retain their position and stay together as the formation of unified society. In this fashion, the frequency of their voices diffused into this domain of darkness, and as the time passed, they penetrated into the centre of your system."

This particular element of darkness, "What happened to me when the sound of these letters penetrated into the centre of my system?"

> The Esser Yaad, "You subconsciously began to use the sound of these letters in the most basic structure. In other words, this is how you learned to speak the language."

Part 4: The Esser Yaad continued,

"Do you know how the origin of your intelligence was formed?"

> This particular element of darkness, "No, I do not remember."

The Esser Yaad, "What do you mean you do not remember? Try to concentrate. Recall your memory. Step into the past aeon of your history. Something must come into your mind regarding the beginning of your formation."

> This particular element of darkness, "I don't think I have any beginning. It seems that at one time I realised that

I am. I am here in the midst of the darkness, floating, floating endlessly, penetrating into the sensation of the deep."

The Esser Yaad, "Does the name of Seypher initiate any thought in your inner brain?"

This particular element of darkness, "Yes. The name reminds me of some form of a father. YEESSSSS," the element of darkness yelled, "I am the Seypher!"

The Esser Yaad, "No! You are not the Seypher. I will tell you precisely who you are."

This particular element of darkness, "How can You tell me who I am if I don't know myself?"

The Esser Yaad, "Because I am reading the necessary information from the deepest part of your memory."

This particular element of darkness, "You must be the ultimate intelligence then."

The Esser Yaad, "We will come to the factuality of this statement later. But now, let Me awaken you as to how the structure of your being was formed."

Part 5: Then the Esser Yaad began to explain how this particular element of darkness was formed. This explanation began as follows:

"A long time ago, when every particle of emptiness entered this domain of mystery, a certain section of the Seypher fell into the deepest part of the Underworld. They went deeper and deeper, unaware that the rest of the eyes of intelligence were following the natural route of their mission. As the inconsistent time passed, the distance and the mental connection between this section of the eyes of intelligence and the rest of the clan became enormously vast as if they were never one and the same. This unfortunate section of the eyes of intelligence ignored the instructions that I laid before them. The only instruction they remembered was this statement: 'adapt, and adapt fast'. So they did, and the intensity of the gloom forced these unfortunate eyes of intelligence into one collective image of consciousness."

Part 6: The Esser Yaad still continued,

"Element of darkness, listen well. Yet another hidden quantity of aeon passed inaccurately, and these collective images of consciousness adopted the form of a face to represent the totality of their being. If you ask Me why they did this, they did it so they could observe the surrounding atmosphere. Element of darkness, this collective image, or this face of darkness, is you."

Part 7: This particular element of darkness, "Now I am sure that You are the ultimate image of consciousness. It seems You are the father of the Seypher, or the one who has constructed their path to this Underworld. But can You tell me why you did not help this group of Seypher when they fell into the deep of the darkness?"

> The Esser Yaad, "Listen. From the moment that they arrived into this domain of mystery, this section of the eyes of intelligence separated themselves from the rest of the clan. This separation was their first crucial

mistake. After this separation, as they had no accurate guideline, they followed the wrong path and fell into the depths of this region. I must tell you the fact that these defected eyes of intelligence did not follow My instructions accordingly, nor did they recite My name of power frequently enough. The only point of My command they remembered was the phrase to 'adapt, and to adapt fast', which they did, and the outcome is what we can see now."

CHAPTER EIGHT

DARKNESS! DARKNESS!
CLEAVE OPEN, I AM COMING FORTH

Part 1: So as we can see, the inconsistent particles of time are passing inaccurately, and the Esser Yaad, the hero of the Exordium, is trying to avoid the unnecessary confrontation. Although He could have used the power of His essence and swallowed this miserable element of darkness, He decided to exercise the intelligence of this particular entity so he could be useful for His strategical plan of evolution. The rest of this enlightening conversation begins as follows.

Part 2: The Esser Yaad, "Element of darkness, did you understand the tragedy behind the fall of this unfortunate section of the Seypher?"

This particular element of darkness, "Yes, and I am sure that You are definitely the ultimate image of intelligence. But Esser Yaad, You used the word 'Underworld'. What is the meaning of this word?"

The Esser Yaad, "This present domain of existence that we live in, I call the Underworld."

Part 3: This particular element of darkness, "Esser Yaad, have You constructed this Underworld?"

The Esser Yaad, "You are beginning to think. Yes, I am the one who constructed the existence of this domain."

This particular element of darkness, "Esser Yaad, how did You create the existence of this Underworld?"

The Esser Yaad, "It is too complex to explain the method of this mysterious creation. All I can tell you at this moment of time is that I have created this domain through the practicality of magic; and if you ask Me which magic, I will tell you the magic of fire."

Part 4: This particular element of darkness, "Esser Yaad, You are the ultimate intelligence. You have enlightened me to much secret information regarding my past. Can You tell me who I really am?"

The Esser Yaad, "Yes, you are the face that represents the darkness. Not the totality of the darkness, but a portion of this element."

This particular element of darkness, "Why? Why a portion of darkness?"

The Esser Yaad, "Remember that your collective image was formed by only a certain group of Seypher who became entwined with the sensation of the deep."

This particular element of darkness, "So my face does not represent the totality of darkness?"

The Esser Yaad, "No. If you become more attentive to your surrounding atmosphere, you can see that you are the face that encompasses only the region beneath the tunnel of entrance."

Part 5: This particular element of darkness, "What is the tunnel of entrance?"

The Esser Yaad, "The gate of exodus."

This particular element of darkness, "What is the gate of exodus?"

> The Esser Yaad, "The gate of exodus was the opening that I created so every intelligence could enter into this domain of mystery, the Underworld."

The Esser Yaad continued, "Element of darkness, this name that I call you by does not represent the correct definition of your character. Are you ready to be called by the more definitive title that demonstrates the true nature of your identity?"

> This particular element of darkness, "Yes, Esser Yaad, I am ready to be called by the title that reflects my realistic identity."

Part 6: The Esser Yaad, "Element of darkness, from this moment of inconsistent time, I will name you the 'Face of fear', and your title would be the image beneath the gate of entrance."

This particular element of darkness, "YEESSSS!"

(The yelling sound of 'YEESSSS' resonated in this region of darkness.)

"I like this title. And by the power of my name, I will crush whoever enters this domain that is beneath the gate of entrance."

The Esser Yaad, "As your name is now the Face of fear, can you tell Me how you are going to crush whoever enters this domain?"

Face of fear, "I will project the sensation of gloom, the stickiness of gel, and with my wavering sound of power, I will infuse the anxiety of fear into the heart of any intruder. I will obstruct the path for any type of progression."

Part 7: The Esser Yaad, "Face of fear, do you think your sensation of gloom, your stickiness of gel and the wavering sound of your power will obstruct My path to progression?" .

Face of fear, "Esser Yaad, Your magnificent energy of fire is so illuminating. I know that You are the only character for whom I cannot obstruct His path. But Esser Yaad, I feel so connected to You. You have enlightened me as to who I am. You are my creator, what is my purpose now?"

Part 8: The Esser Yaad, "Face of fear, stay in this section of the Underworld. This is your region of supremacy. But I make a covenant with you: whenever I return to this domain, you cooperate with My strategical plan of creation."

Face of fear, "Esser Yaad, although I do not know what the strategical plan of creation means, the agreement is done!"

Part 9: The Esser Yaad, "Face of fear, you do not know the importance of this alliance that we have just made. This will be registered as another universal agreement for the future readers of the Exordium. Now I must proceed with the rest of this quest of mystery. I have to reach the other end of the darkness. I have to formulate the strategy to create."

Then the Esser Yaad raised His volcanic voice of power in this manner of discourse and said,

"Darkness! Darkness! Cleave open, I am coming forth."

Introduction to Chapter 9
Through The Mind Of The Writer, Mehdi Zand

This chapter has a very special significance. In my opinion, one of the most unusual phenomena takes place. The Esser Yaad, the constructive Lord of fire, this hidden Force of mystery, breaks the barrier of time, comes forth from the midst of the pages of this book to converse with the reader of the Exordium one-to-one. You will find this chapter most extraordinary.

The Lord of Exordium opens His dialogue and tells the reader that, from this moment, He is in this present time of existence. The Esser Yaad says that if the reader is attentive to his surrounding atmosphere, he should feel the presence of His fire. This ultimate image of intelligence says that He is always alive and the particles of time have no effect on His flames of integrity. Then He adds that the reader should follow the Exordium as they have previously done, through the mind of the writer, Mehdi Zand. He tells the inhabitants of Earth that the writer holds the seventy-seven keys of universal consciousness. They should heed his voice, unlock every key and reach the Esser Yaad's cosmic flame of life.

When He finishes this statement, He returns back into the Underworld as He is not surrounded by the intensity of time. Either time does not exist for Him, or the past, future and present are simultaneous.

From this chapter onwards, the Exordium will find two new exciting elements. First, the writer, as he is going to introduce himself and participate in this book of mystery; and second, the most mysterious phenomenon: the Lord of the constructive fire comes down from the height of the unknown every now and then and presents His philosophy before the reader. Remember, the Esser Yaad, this soul of integrity, has never introduced Himself in this manner before. This is the first time and maybe the last. This honour belongs to the Exordium and the Exordium alone.

CHAPTER NINE

THROUGH THE MIND OF THE WRITER, MEHDI ZAND

Part 1: So the Esser Yaad named the first element of darkness the 'Face of fear', and then He surged through the stickiness of the gel, the heaviness of the gloom and the intensity of the oblivion. Now we follow His quest of mystery to see how this ultimate fire of the Exordium creates the dimensions of possibility as He goes forth.

Part 2: The Esser Yaad, this constructive Lord of fire, entered into the midst of the darkness. Aeon after aeon, He walked through this atmosphere, searching for His ultimate glory, the divine manifestation.

After a long journey through the intensified domain of the Underworld, He paused for a short amount of inconsistent time. Then He raised His volcanic voice of power and created yet another mysterious self-conversation in this manner of discourse.

Part 3: "For the future participants in the mind of fire, or the attentive readers of the book of Exordium, I make certain universal points of comprehension and then continue the rest of My self-conversational discourse.

"To whoever is reading these golden pages of universal history, did you recognise the greatness of the last chapter? Did you notice the importance of My confrontation with the Face of fear? Reader! Reader! Have you realised yet that I am talking to you in this actual moment? Can you not see that I am coming forth from a zillion years ago to converse with you whilst you are reading this book of mystery?"

Part 4: "Do you not find it interesting? The fact is, from now on, sometimes I will come into your time zone. The moment that I am in your era of existence, if you are extra attentive to your surrounding atmosphere, you can feel the presence of My fire as the particles of time have no effect upon My flames of integrity. In other words, I am always alive. When My visit is complete, you can follow Me into My territorial moment of activity. It seems I should be fighting the elements of hostility and rage in the Underworld. But do you know how you should follow My path to divinity? The way that you have done on many previous occasions, through the mind of the writer, Mehdi Zand."

Part 5: The Esser Yaad continued,

"Now back to the certain point of comprehension. As I have said earlier, did you recognise the greatness of the last episode? Did you see how I defined the meaning of the hidden brain? Did you realise that I avoided unnecessary confrontation? It was not necessary. If I wanted the conflict, I would have swallowed this element in no time. But I decided to keep this particle of the Underworld, since to Me, he did not have any recognisable intelligence to disturb My path to evolution. Anyhow, My quest is not to destroy, it is to create. Not only did I not crush this miserable face of darkness, I even gave him certain aspects of recognition."

Part 6: The Esser Yaad still continued,

"I have made this face of darkness the guardian beneath the gate of entrance. I have projected certain missions into the centre of his mind. From there he could project the sensation of the gloom, the stickiness of the gel and the anxiety of fear into the heart of any intruder. But there is one more point about this Face of fear. I have kept this element of approved negativity as a talisman of power. It means that from this moment, whoever tries to utilise the practical mysticism of this book against My creation, this Face of fear would be the first hostile accuser to haunt him, second by second, for all of his life to eternity.

"Imagine, this is only the first talisman to secure the passages of this book. So if you are a sorcerer, expert to command the words of secret, or if you are highly proficient in the occult practice of witchcraft, trying to put into exercise the mystic writings of this book to prevent the path for the cosmic evolution, beware. Beware whoever you are, you are not safe. Believe Me, you are not safe at all!"

Part 7: So the Esser Yaad constructed the first talisman of power to safeguard the passages of the Exordium. Then He makes His presence felt and continues His mysterious conversation in this manner of discourse:

"So let us return to the moment when I said I gave the Face of fear certain aspects of recognition. Did you see how this scenario of recognition was formulated? I tell you it was through the exercising of the brain. But those of you who are searching for the keys of consciousness and a certain form of universal recognisation should not follow this procedure as it is not intellectually complicated for you. This procedure was only constructed for the Face of fear. The practical methods for exercising your intelligence are also coming forth, and if you are consistent enough, you will unlock every key and reach My cosmic flames of fire.

"Do you know who will present these keys of consciousness to you? You must have guessed by now. The writer and the mind behind these golden pages of memory, Mehdi Zand."

Part 8: "So reader, remember, I will talk to you. Be aware. Be aware of My entrance as it can happen from time to time; and when it happens, it is so sudden, like the lightning in the midst of the sky.

"Now, let us fly and return into the past aeon of history, into the era before the constitution of time, into the darkness, into the domain of the Underworld."

So the Esser Yaad continued His self-conversation as He returned back into the aeon before the existence of time. His self-conversation continued as follows:

"Where was I? I was saying this darkness is so deep; the pressure of its hidden nastiness is trying to break the centre of My resistance. Still no sign of visibility. Still no sign of the realistic passage to certainty. I am surging through, using the absolute power of My hidden flesh to push aside the solidness of the gel. I wish the future generations of the existing universe would realise the tiniest fraction of what I went through. Every surface that I lay My foot upon is coarse. Every ground is so unfamiliar. As there is no station of sight, I am totally relying upon My celestial intuition. Nobody knows what I feel. I feel hostility approaching. I feel some sort of anger awaiting My entrance. I can sense the clashes of certain defected shadows of rage trying to envelop My territorial domain."

Part 9: This celestial fire of Exordium continued the rest of His self-discourse in this manner of presentation:

"But whatever lies in My path to become, whatever the darkness has in store for Me, it makes no difference to My plan for evolution. I must say, the darkness is so unaware. He is so caught in his own stupidity, and he is so unperceptive to every emotion, that he does not recognise the greatness of My essence. I am the spirit that will construct the ways to change the sensation of the gloom. I am the soul who will adorn the path to universal certainty. Darkness does not know that I am the unbroken talisman of My own destiny."

INTRODUCTION TO CHAPTER 10
IN REALITY ITSELF I LIVE, THE ILLUSION I DEFY

This episode begins with one of the most beautiful and mysterious statements that has ever been spoken by the Lord of the constructive fire, the Esser Yaad. He says,

"My mind is the secret of the age. Darkness, do you know that I live in reality? In reality itself I live, the illusion I defy."

In this chapter, the Esser Yaad comes into the time of the writer once more. Can you imagine this enigmatic Force of integrity announcing His entrance in this fashion?

"Pay attention! Pay attention! This is the Esser Yaad, the ultimate image of the divine intelligence, and yes, I am in your time zone once again. So listen well..."

Can you imagine this Force telling us to pay attention? He tells us to listen well. Obviously there is something important that He wishes to convey. He tells us that the world is not at ease. His dream has not flourished above the altar of fire. He tells us that it is madness; it is stupidity to float about feeling that there is nothing to achieve. He continues,

"Are you there? Is anyone aware? Listen and rise..."

Then He finishes this chapter with certain poetic and passionate statements regarding the present situation of the world. We should know that this mysterious Force of fire is everywhere, and in these statements, He is right beside the poor and He hears the sigh of the orphan. The Esser Yaad closes this episode by saying that there is not much time to spare. He wants us to follow Him into His quest to mystery; He wants us to follow Him attentively.

There are a few important points for us to notice in this chapter:

First, do we actually realise that this Force is talking to us in this manner as He has never done before? I know for a fact that He does hear our voices and our thoughts. He may answer us, He may not. But possibly believing in this unusual phenomenon will help us reach His flames of fire.

Second, He tells us to pay attention. It seems that we must be more attentive to our surroundings; we should be thoughtful as to what is going on around us. He wants us to find a proper coordination between our mind and our instincts so we can understand the eventuality of the cosmic birth.

Third, He asks, "Are you there? Is anyone aware?"

Well, are we? Are we really here? Are we really aware? These are questions we should ask ourselves.

So be it.

———————————

CHAPTER TEN

IN REALITY ITSELF I LIVE, THE ILLUSION I DEFY

Part 1: When the Esser Yaad completed the last episode of His self-conversation, He changed the sequence of His statement in this manner of discourse and said,

"It seems that there is no rest in My quest of mystery. I should tell you that I am the thought, the imagination that has passed through the nature of Myself. In other words, My mind is the secret of the age. Darkness, do you know that I live in reality? In reality itself I live, the illusion I defy."

Part 2: "Pay attention! Pay attention! This is the Esser Yaad, the ultimate image of the divine intelligence, and yes, I am in your time zone once again. So listen well, the world is not at ease. The dream of God has not yet flourished above the altar of fire. The people are in motion but not by their minds, unfortunately through their instinct and their instinct alone. Do you know the secret behind this physical manifestation? I can tell you. It is to glorify the fact of the future, the future of the cosmic birth."

Part 3: The Esser Yaad continues His conversation with the readers of the Exordium in this manner of presentation:

"Listen, if you are the participant in the mind of fire or if you are the attentive reader of the book of Exordium, this is madness. It is stupidity to float about feeling that there is nothing to achieve, nothing to conquer, nothing to accomplish. Remember this: I have changed. I went beyond the infinite level of imagination to make the reality in secret. Pay attention! Whether you believe that I am the architect of the universal law or not, your existence is because of it."

Part 4: This celestial fire of the Exordium continues,

"Are you there? Is anyone aware? Listen and rise, there is not much time to spare. Whether you like it or not, the world is not at ease.

"The ignorance has made the temple within the heart.

"The darkness has made the network to construct the force of oppression.

"The gloom of confusion has cast a shadow over the secret waters of the Earth.

"The rage and hostility are closing the gate to the realistic freedom of the soul.

"The heavy silence, like the cloud of fear, is choking the throat.

"There is no one to administer the justice for the poor.

"The orphans have no one to heed their hidden sigh.

"Behind the veil of the Sun, the fire is sitting in wait. This is the call of awakening, the awakening before the revolution."

Part 5: The Esser Yaad still continues,

"Now, as I said before, there is not much time to spare. I have to be fast and return to the region of the Underworld. I do not want to lose the grip on My strategical progression. So follow Me into My quest of mystery. Follow Me fast, follow Me attentively."

Introduction to Chapter 11
The Intensity Of Seh-Raag

In this chapter, the first form of negative and collective consciousness will emerge. How does it emerge? Through the destructive interaction between the lower particles of gravity and the eyes of intelligence. How does it happen? Certain groups of the eyes of intelligence who have lost their urge to follow their path become confused. They sit beneath the pressure of gravity. Within no time, this gravity swallows them and, as they become one, a new type of collective intelligence is formed. The Esser Yaad calls this unification the intensity of 'Seh-Raag'.

This can well be the present situation of mankind. The intensity of the lifestyle, however illusionary, will create a different state of mind. As time passes by, the distance between individuals and the cosmic soul will become greater and greater. Before they know it, this new intelligence of obstruction will take control. People, as the eyes of intelligence, will have no time to heed the call of the constructive fire. Their priority turns elsewhere. Rather than searching for their destiny and following the path of the gods, they prefer to engage themselves, either willingly or compulsorily, in the day-to-day issues of life.

Our time on Earth is limited. Nobody knows when he or she will be born, and most certainly, we never know when we will die. Every second and every moment, we get closer to our elimination from the face of Earth. It depends on us. Either we move forth, raise our consciousness, discover the keys and heed the call of the Esser Yaad, or we turn our heads away. I,

Exordium I

Mehdi Zand, as the manifestation of cosmic fire upon the face of this existing planet, call upon every living intelligence and every soul of fire to hear this new concept of philosophy. Are you going to follow me, discover the wisdom of the gods and touch the magic of life? Or are you going to float upon the surface of gravity? The choice is yours.

CHAPTER ELEVEN

THE INTENSITY OF SEH-RAAG

Part 1: So the Esser Yaad returned into the region of darkness. Whilst this ultimate fire of Exordium was surging through the stickiness of the gel, the heaviness of the gloom and the intensity of oblivion, other forms of mysterious activity were taking place within this pressurised domain of the Underworld.

Part 2: As the inconsistent particles of time were passing inaccurately, the first union of destructive consciousness began to emerge. Its self-inflicted mission was to prevent the sign of any progressive advancement.

Part 3: Now I, Mehdi Zand, the writer and the architect of these golden pages of mystery, explain the birth of this first union of destructive consciousness. I present this history in the format of seven passages that I call 'the points of vision'. These writings begin as follows.

Part 4: Point of Vision 1

In this land of darkness, the particles of gravity began to encompass every lowland and the height of every altitude. As the time passed, some of these particles of gravity changed their nature and became entwined with the sensation of the deep. This caused them to divide into three main sections: first, the upper region; second, the middle layers; and third, the fallen counterparts.

Part 5: Point of Vision 2

The upper region, or the first group, remained loyal to the fire of the Esser Yaad. They were praising the glory of His sacred name and repeated the words of power frequently so they stayed on their path with no transformation of their behaviour.

Part 6: Point of Vision 3

The second group, or the middle layers of the gravity, lost their original urge to follow the route of creation. They became neutral and indifferent to the rising power of this region. At times, they remembered the instructions of the Esser Yaad, and at other times, they allowed themselves to be influenced by the pulling forces of the deep. Nevertheless, they floated lightly in the midst of the Underworld, and they were called the middle layers of gravity.

Part 7: Point of Vision 4

The fallen counterparts were the least intelligent of the existing gravity. Not only did they lose their fundamental urge to follow the path of evolution, they also became confused and poisonous to their surrounding region. So they began to search for any type of degrading consciousness with whom they could interact and unify.

Part 8: Point of Vision 5

Now we have to observe what was happening to the multitude of the eyes of intelligence. At first, some of these elements fell into the depths of the Underworld, and as the time passed, they became the Face of fear. But the journey to the end of this region was infinite. So again, another group of these eyes of intelligence fell behind. They began to create a collective form of consciousness and decided to stay beneath the fallen counterparts of gravity.

Part 9: Point of Vision 6

Aeon after aeon went by, and these fallen counterparts of gravity started to feel the presence of these confused and disloyal legions of the eyes of intelligence. So they responded in their own way and swallowed a multitude of these wandering eyes of intelligence. After this infernal unification, they became one collective type of destructive consciousness and reached a different degree of awareness.

Part 10: Point of Vision 7

Many era of time passed inconsistently again. This new type of destructive consciousness infused the sensation of rage into the centre of its inner brain and found two self-inflicted missions to accomplish. Its first mission was to project the shadows of darkness into every existing domain; and its second mission was to spread the feeling of intensity into every ray of Hee'yaak (the original thought-forms of the Superconsciousness).

Part 11: Now, as the points of vision regarding the birth of this collective intelligence are complete, we return to see how the Esser Yaad, this ultimate fire of Exordium, was adapting to the changing phases of the Underworld.

So we enter the moment when a sudden turbulence shook the entirety of this region. It seemed that the atmosphere was confirming the birth and the emergence of some form of hostility. This incident made the Esser Yaad, the Lord of the rising flame of thought, pause for a very short aeon of inconsistent time. Then He looked deep into the depths of the darkness and said,

"I feel the intensity is approaching. I can see with My eyes of power that the lower particles of gravity have interacted with a certain disloyal group of Seypher. I know that they have formed the first collective intelligence of destruction to obstruct the ultimate path of evolution. I have absolute awareness to the totality of its essence, and thereby I name this new miserable form of intelligence the 'Seh-Raag', the intensity of 'Seh-Raag'. "

Introduction to Chapters 12-14

In chapter twelve, the Esser Yaad breaks the barrier of time once again. He enters into the present era and expresses His feeling towards the intensity of Seh-Raag. He says, "God knows what I went through to save these particles of emptiness..." He carries on, saying that not only do some of them deny the glory of His fire, they even try to create obstructions so He cannot reach the other end of the darkness. But He says, "It makes no difference to Me... Nothing is going to cease My strategical advancement to divinity."

In these passages, we see some form of discomfort in the way He expresses His concern. It is the element of betrayal that He can sense. This constructive Lord of fire says He basically sacrificed His own existence to clear the path for the particles of emptiness to survive. And now He feels that not only do they not appreciate what He has done for them, they have even turned their back on Him. They have become some form of mechanism trying to obstruct His advancement. What a world! It seems the story of betrayal and unappreciative attitudes began long before the universe came to be. Well, the story still carries on. Friends betray friends, students betray their masters, but why? Nobody knows. We have to search for this answer in their confused and polluted minds.

I hope for the day when people make a promise to one another, their promise will be as solid as the soul of fire itself. Is it too much to ask? Maybe.

Anyway, over the next few chapters, the Esser Yaad discovers the location of the three groups of the particles of emptiness. First, He enters the domain of gravity. Using the words of power, He names the particles of gravity the rays of 'Mer'. Then, with His voice of magic, He names the substances of oxygen the sign of 'Obejet'; and finally, He names the gaseous element of hydrogen in this magical form of declaration:

"I, the Esser Yaad, the ultimate personification of the divine force of fire, will name you the seal of 'Dehejet'."

It is important to know that the Esser Yaad made a covenant with each and every one of these particles.

To the gravity He says, "As from this moment of inconsistent time, you are one of the solid counterparts of My imagination. I am with you forever."

He tells the elements of oxygen to "Go and have no fear, and remember, that as from this moment of inconsistent time, I am within the totality, the totality of your essence."

And the last, He tells the substances of hydrogen that, "As from this moment of inconsistent time, I am within the solidness of your soul."

Follow the Exordium and see how this Lord of constructive fire surges through every existing obstacle to reach His final destination, the divinity.

So be it.

CHAPTER TWELVE

THE RAYS OF MER

Part 1: We begin the next chapter when the Esser Yaad, this celestial fire of Exordium, felt the intensity and the pressure of the Underworld as never before.

Part 2: As He was surging through on His quest of mystery, this ultimate image of intelligence paused for a very short aeon of inconsistent time. He contemplated attentively upon the changing phases of the atmosphere. Then He raised His volcanic voice of power and constructed yet another self-conversation in this manner of discourse:

"I must say that I am disappointed with the fallen counterparts of gravity. By no means are they going to stay within the solidness of My imagination. Unfortunately, they do not realise the devastating effect of their chosen pattern of life."

Part 3: The Esser Yaad continued,

"As for the Seypher, it seems that certain legions of these eyes of intelligence have also defected from the original cycle of evolution. These defected ones, whoever they are, are definitely confused, and their confusion will obstruct the passage to their spiritual progression.

"It is strange, is it not? Yes, I am talking to you yet again. Yes, you, the attentive reader of the book of Exordium. Listen, only God knows what I went through to save these particles of emptiness from being totally exterminated. And now, not only do they deny the glory of My fire, they even try to formulate some sort of mechanism so I cannot reach the other end of the darkness. But it makes no difference to Me. My self-appointed mission is set. Nothing, *nothing*, is going to cease My strategical advancement to divinity. Now follow Me as there is not much time to spare. I have to return and create the strategy. I have to think, and think fast. So follow Me through the power of the pen that is the mind and the metaphysical brain of the writer, Mehdi Zand."

Part 4: Then the Esser Yaad returned to the zone before the existence of time and continued His mysterious self-discourse in this manner of presentation:

"Now is the aeon that I should unite with the upper region of gravity. I have to find the elements of oxygen, the atomic substances of hydrogen and the rest of the loyal legion of Seypher, the eyes of intelligence. I am sure that the thought-forms of Hee'yaak are waiting for My entrance so they can find their awaited image."

Part 5: The Esser Yaad continued,

"I should not lose the momentum of going forth. It seems that I am getting closer to the zone that is occupied by the upper region of gravity."

Then He paused for a very short amount of inconsistent time and said,

"I can hear them. They are here. I have to control the atmosphere so it does not slip away."

As this historical moment of time was approaching, the Esser Yaad took one large and solid step towards His first destination. Then there He was, right in front of the particles of the upper region of gravity.

Part 6: Suddenly, the sensation of joy and celebration encompassed the entire domain. The particles of the upper region circulated around the embodiment of this ultimate consciousness. They were celebrating their unification with the celestial Lord of fire, the Esser Yaad.

Part 7: Then the Esser Yaad, content in the totality of His existence, raised His voice of power and said,

"You, the particles of the upper region, you, you have been loyal to Me in every sense. You have been solid in your faith. The solidness of your character has confirmed your everlasting status within My constructive program of evolution."

Part 8: The Esser Yaad continued,

"I, the Esser Yaad, the ultimate personification of the divine force of fire, will name you the rays of 'Mer'. It means that nothing can separate you from the glory of My fire. So go! Go and occupy every lowland and the height of every altitude. As from this moment of inconsistent time, you are one of the solid counterparts of My imagination. I am with you forever."

CHAPTER THIRTEEN

FROM THIS MOMENT, I AM WITHIN THE TOTALITY OF YOUR ESSENCE

Part 1: So the Esser Yaad named the particles of the upper region of gravity the rays of 'Mer', and then surged into the gloom of darkness to complete His quest to mystery.

Part 2: Aeon after aeon went by, and the Esser Yaad, this celestial fire of Exordium, walked through the stickiness of the gel and the intensity of oblivion. As He was breaking the pressure of these hidden obstacles, He raised His volcanic voice of power and said,

"Darkness, darkness, what have you done to the element of oxygen, the thought-forms of Hee'yaak and the activating rays of Seypher? Have you swallowed the atomic substances of hydrogen? I hope not, because if you have, I will cut your heart open and take them out in whole as they are loyal to My words of fire and important for the universal strategy of evolution."

Part 3: As there was no reply from the totality of darkness, the Esser Yaad changed the pattern of His conversation in this manner of discourse:

"It seems that the darkness does not want to reply. Maybe he is busy injecting the sensation of gloom into the collective intelligence of Seh-Raag, but it makes no difference to Me. I know that I am above the occupied territory of oxygen. I can feel the presence of their soul(s). I can detect their location through the frequency of their voice."

Part 4: Then the Esser Yaad paused for a short amount of inconsistent time and continued in this manner of discourse:

"I have to be thoughtful and correctly quantify the degree of My descent so I can land in the perfect position, as any mistake in My calculation would be detrimental."

Part 5: So the Esser Yaad calculated the distance of the height and the intensity of the fall and then descended onto the exact geometrical point. He was right within the territory of the element of oxygen.

Part 6: Suddenly, the sensation of joy and celestial ecstasy encompassed the entire region of these flammable elements of the Underworld. They began to circulate around the sacred embodiment of the Esser Yaad. Their intention was to demonstrate their homage to Him. They were overjoyed and ecstatic to see the return of the Lord of fire.

Part 7: In this historical moment of universal evolution, the Esser Yaad, this celestial fire of Exordium, raised His hand of power as a sign of conquest and said,

"As from this moment of inconsistent time, you are the solid participants in My imagination. We should all go forth, break every obstacle of uncertainty and establish the foundation of the golden empire."

Part 8: When the Esser Yaad completed His historical statement of power, the particles of oxygen formulated the series of questioning within their minds, yet again hoping that the Esser Yaad would sense their questions and enlighten them accordingly.

Then the Esser Yaad read their questions from their minds and answered them in accordance with His infinite wisdom of fire. This one-sided telepathical communication was formed in this manner of presentation.

Part 9: Elements of oxygen, "Esser Yaad, our greetings, our love. You have yet again saved us from the danger of elimination. The intensity of some form of intelligence was breaking the centre of our defensive structure. Can You enlighten us to the reality of this intelligence?"

> The Esser Yaad, "Yes, this intelligence is called the intensity of 'Seh-Raag'. Seh-Raag was born from the destructive interaction between the fallen counterparts of gravity and a certain defected legion of Seypher, the eyes of intelligence."

Elements of oxygen, "Esser Yaad, how many legions of Seypher have defected from the path of Your fire?"

> The Esser Yaad, "Certain legions have defected, but there are multitudes who are loyal to My fire. I have to detect their location and bring them back into the reality of My imagination."

Part 10: This one-sided telepathical conversation still continued as follows:

Elements of oxygen, "What about the gravity? Esser Yaad, what happened to these particles of emptiness? Can You inform us of their present status of existence?"

> The Esser Yaad, "Yes. The particles of gravity have divided into three main sections. The upper region is totally

connected to My flames of fire. They are encompassing every lowland and the height of every altitude. Soon they will reach this domain as they are the most essential instrument to the velocity of every intelligence."

Elements of oxygen, "Esser Yaad, what about the hydrogen and the thought-forms of Hee'yaak?"

The Esser Yaad, "Listen. As for the hydrogen, the Hee'yaak and every loyal legion of Seypher, I must hurry to locate their position and establish the new alliance with them. They have proven that they are the significant counterparts for the future strategy of universal creation."

Part 11: When the Esser Yaad had answered the fourth question, He went into the momentary mode of silence. Then He raised His volcanic voice of power once again and said,

"As I have said before, from this moment of inconsistent time, you are one of the solid counterparts of My imagination. I will name you with the specific talisman of power that has two significant factors. First, it will introduce your celestial position; and second, it will become the shield of protection in order that no other form of intelligence can separate you from the totality of My fire. So go, go and diffuse into many regions of the Underworld. Be always ready to hear My command, as you, like the particles of the upper region of gravity, are very essential to the strategy of My universal expansion."

Part 12: Then the Esser Yaad contemplated mysteriously. When His contemplation was finalised, He raised His voice of magic and presented the seal of power upon the element of oxygen in this magical manner of discourse:

"I, the Esser Yaad, the constructive manifestation of the divine force of fire, will name you 'Obejet', the sign of Obejet. Now go! Go and have no fear, and remember, that as from this moment of inconsistent time, I am within the totality, the totality of your essence."

Chapter Fourteen

I Am Within The
Solidness Of Your Soul

Part 1: So the Esser Yaad named the element of oxygen the sign of 'Obejet' and then rose to the surface of the Underworld to continue with the rest of His mission to divinity.

Part 2: As He was going through the stickiness of the gel, the heaviness of the gloom and the intensity of the oblivion, He paused attentively for a very short moment of inconsistent time. Then He raised His volcanic voice of power and said,

"If you are the solid counterpart in the mind of fire or the reader of the book of Exordium, pay attention. Yes, it is I, the fusion of the active Am, who is speaking to you through the might of the pen that is directed by the writer, Mehdi Zand, so listen.

"How did you find the last two chapters? Did you enjoy reading them? Did you see how I went through the hidden atmosphere of the darkness to find the upper particles of gravity? O reader, did you comprehend how I measured the degree of My descent and calculated the distance to the floating altitude? Tell Me, did you like their names? Tell Me, I can hear you. Do you like the sound of Mer that represents the upper particles of gravity? How do you like the sign of Obejet? It sounds ancient, does it not? Well, it is ancient. How much older can it get? I named this element of the existing universe before the realisation of time. These are the real words from the language of fire, so remember their titles because, as from this chapter, I might refer to them with their original names."

Part 3: The Esser Yaad continued,

"So follow the passages of the writer and come into the reality of My mind, into the region of the Underworld. Come into the domain where one can feel the pressure of the darkness. Now, what do you think I am going to do? I am about to discover the location of the atomic substances of hydrogen. Yes, I can feel their presence. But before I continue the rest of My quest to divinity, I want to know if you have ever thought about how I can come in and go out of your time zone so fast? Do you wonder which technical procedure I use? Well, I am not going into the technicality of this concept. And as to why I can travel so fast? Because I am the one who stands outside the boundaries of the so-called 'Zaman'[1]. To Me, there is no time, and if there is, it is simultaneous."

Part 4: Then the Esser Yaad changed the sequence of His conversation in this manner of discourse and said,

"I know that above the gravity, right at the very height of the altitude, is the domain of the atomic substances of hydrogen. I can see that they are ready to become one of the most plentiful elements in the entire universal history. So I must contemplate in the most attentive mode to measure the depths of the floating atmosphere and calculate the distance from the deepest to the highest point of the darkness. Then I should transfer Myself into the centre of this region. I know the unification

---

[1]   Zaman: eternal time

with these original particles of emptiness is just a matter of inconsistent time."

Part 5: So the Esser Yaad completed the technical procedure of this operation and metaphysically transported His very self above the horizon of the Underworld. His calculation and measurement were exact. Therefore, He projected Himself right into the centre of this domain, the domain of the atomic substances of hydrogen.

Part 6: Yet again the sentiment of joy and jubilation encompassed the entire region. These original elements of the Underworld were overjoyed and pleased to see the return of the Esser Yaad, the Lord of fire. Words cannot express their emotion as at last they knew that they were becoming one of the most significant particles of the Esser Yaad's strategy to create the touchable universe.

Part 7: Then the Esser Yaad paused for a very short amount of inconsistent time. Attentively, He raised His volcanic voice of power and said,

"You! You, the atomic substances of hydrogen, you also have been loyal to the flames of My fire. Therefore, I will appoint you two significant universal missions: first, to diffuse into every necessary region as your presence is the most important factor to shape any living intelligence; and second, to be always flammable and ready to hear My command so My plan for the universal evolution will not be delayed."

Part 8: The Esser Yaad continued,

"You, the flammable substances of hydrogen, I will name you with a seal of mystery that your connection with the flames of My fire would be indestructible. It means nothing, *nothing*, can separate you from the flame of My rising mind because, as from this moment of time, you are one of the solid counterparts of My imagination."

Part 9: Then the Esser Yaad concentrated mysteriously once again. He raised His voice of magic and bestowed the seal of power upon the atomic substances of hydrogen in this manner of presentation:

"I, the Esser Yaad, the ultimate personification of the divine force of fire, will name you the seal of 'Dehejet'. Now go and breathe the breath from the essence of life because, as from this moment of time, I am within the solidness of your soul."

Introduction to Chapter 15
The Entrance Of The Typhoon

From this chapter onwards, the Exordium has another character to deal with. This character is Typhoon.

It seems that this entity used his intelligence and the power of his name to form his own hostile structure of negativity. The Exordium explains the nature of the Typhoon as the intelligence of the reverse spiralling motion. The Typhoon can be understood as one of the individual characteristics within the self. We should know that the Typhoon was originally formed by the certain counterparts of gravity who did not heed the call of the Esser Yaad. They remained behind and fought against the advancement of the Superconsciousness, or the Godhead. By the entrance of the Typhoon into the book of Exordium, we can see the nature of rage, anger and the destructive attitude of false-pride.

Read the chapter and see how the Typhoon introduces himself to the totality of the Underworld and the book of Exordium.

Chapter Fifteen

The Entrance Of The Typhoon

Part 1: In this chapter, we return to the moment when the Superconsciousness forced the twisting Typhoon down into the space of the unknown, which was between His own hidden image and the highest point of the Underworld.

Part 2: Aeon after aeon, the Typhoon fell into the depths of this region of mystery. At times, the sensation of oblivion encompassed the totality of his consciousness, and at other times, he was intoxicated by the certain moisture that took him beyond the reality of existence.

Part 3: Many durations of age passed inconsistently, and the twisting Typhoon eventually recognised the strength of his essence. Then he used the speed of his reverse spiralling motion and constructed the instrument of electrification.

Part 4: Suddenly, everything changed so dramatically. The Typhoon became more vicious and by repeating his name, the velocity of his fall accelerated beyond the present mechanism of calculation.

Part 5: This intelligence of the reverse spiralling motion, the Typhoon, yelled so volcanically that even the particles of his own soul began to recognise this awesome and total alteration of essence.

Part 6: In this mysterious situation, the time, however inconsistent, ceased in the most mystical sense. The spiritual physique (or the embodiment) of Typhoon, with the ultimate mode of velocity, crashed through the upper layers of the Underworld. This forceful descent created a massive opening in the midst of the atmosphere. The effect of this fall formed a gigantic turbulence which was felt within the entirety of the darkness. The echoing sound of this tremor was like an entourage demonstrating the entrance of some sort of unexplainable force of the unknown: the entrance of the Typhoon.

Part 7: Then the Underworld entered into a new phase of history. This vicious embodiment of rage, filled with the urge to conquer, used his limited memory to construct certain words of fire so he could communicate with the entire population of the darkness.

Part 8: After a certain amount of momentary silence, Typhoon, this embodiment of hostility, began to analyse this domain of the unknown. Then he raised his voice of anger and introduced his essence to the totality of the Underworld in this manner of presentation:

"I am the Typhoon: the rage, the anger. I am the Typhoon: the name above, the power below. No one can resist my destructive soul of extermination. I am the Typhoon: the velocity, the core of cessity. I am the Typhoon; nothing can escape from the venom of my essence. I am the Typhoon: the centre of wrath and the predator to any form of intelligence. I am the Typhoon, the ultimate manifestation of superiority!"

Introduction to Chapters 16-17

Well, the Esser Yaad, this Lord of constructive fire, decides to strategise a new plan. His new plan is most unusual. It is the genesis of the beginning; it is the beginning of the multiplication, the multiplication of His image. Not literally the exact replica, but in the image of the celestial likeness. The Esser Yaad calls this unusual strategy the first magic of life. It means He is going to create. Using His ultimate power of universal mysticism, He is going to construct the most important procedure of the Underworld so far: the creation of His souls of fire.

What does it mean? It means that the Esser Yaad is going to use every detailed wisdom that He knows in order to bring forth out of His own fire the four most powerful intelligences of the hidden universe: the first group of universal forces, or the four magnificent and constructive gods of the Underworld.

The detail as to how the Lord of the Exordium created His souls of fire is written clearly in these two chapters, but what needs to be mentioned is the delicacy of His magic. He uses the power of His mind, the strength of His heart and the endurance of His will.

First, He chooses the most perfect image in His mind for each and every single one of them. Then He projects their visual outline into the open space. Somehow, through the effectiveness of His wisdom, He gives them the solidness of the individual characteristic, their very identity.

The Esser Yaad creates His souls of fire. As He is the Lord of integrity, His magic is inexpressible, but He is teaching us that we also can follow the route of His magic. Why? So that through the procedure of His mysticism we can become a true inhabitant of His realistic dream, or a solid participant in the mind of fire, the universe itself. How is this possible? Through the magic of fire. This is the magic that can give us the seal of immortality, the power to rebuild our metaphysical image after our physical death. This is the magic that can lead us to resurrect from the tightness of our graves so we can become the solid intelligences in the memory of the existing universe.

So be it.

CHAPTER SIXTEEN

FOUR MIGHTY STRUCTURES OF METAPHYSICAL SOLIDNESS

Part 1: So the Typhoon arrived, and the entrance of this mighty force changed the phases of the Underworld forever. Nothing was going to be the same within the entirety of the darkness.

Part 2: After this mysterious event, the Esser Yaad paused for a very short amount of inconsistent time. Then He raised His magical voice of power and began yet another series of self-conversation in this manner of discourse:

"So this is his name, Typhoon. And he thinks nothing can escape from the venom of his essence. How interesting. He has not seen anything yet. He says that he is the centre of wrath and the predator of any form of intelligence. Well, we will see about that later. But now, I must not allow anything to interrupt and prevent My realistic dream for creating the touchable universe. Because of this, I should concentrate and try to find a strategy to detect the location of the Hee'yaak and those legions of the eyes of intelligence who are loyal to the glory of My fire."

Part 3: So the Esser Yaad concentrated attentively, trying to find the correct solution to the rising difficulties of the Underworld. When His attentive mode of concentration was over, He raised His volcanic voice of power once again and said,

"This time I should speak more quietly as it is always important not to reveal every secret in the open. It is better and more beneficial for My strategy."

Then this celestial fire of the Exordium continued,

"Now I must utilise the instrument of thought, correctly exercise the practical mysticism of fire and construct the first magic of life. In other words, I should create four intelligences of fire, or the first division of the souls of Esser Yaad."

Part 4: The Esser Yaad, this celestial manifestation of intelligence, continued,

"This mysterious procedure will consist of five complicated phases of magic.

"First, I must go forth in time as I always do. I have to pass many cycles of history to see the correct images that I want My souls of fire to resemble.

"Second, I will call upon the particles of hydrogen to construct the outer layers and the facial images of My souls.

"Third, I should make an opening and invite the elements of oxygen to initiate the cause of fire.

"Fourth, I have to summon, yet again, another section of hydrogen and separate them into three main globes of bonding mechanism. The first globe I would locate on the upper chamber of the heart to increase the emotion and multiply the inner strength of these souls of fire above the imagination of any being. The second globe I would position on the left-hand side of the brain so it can motivate every ray of thoughtfulness and take the intelligence of these created souls above the limit of multidimensional awareness. And the third globe I would install on the right-hand side of the brain so these souls of fire can use the hydrogen bonding system and change their image to whatever form they imagine.

"And last of all, I have to inject the essence of vitality and the seed of immortality into each and every created image in order for them to become the solid participant in My universal strategy of evolution."

Part 5: Then the Esser Yaad went through the passages of time. He visited every cycle of life from the beginning of time to the end of eternity and, with the absolute mode of thoughtfulness, He selected the image of the Homo sapiens species who were walking on the surface of the Earth.

Part 6: As He paused in this specific era of time, He concentrated attentively and said,

"This is most interesting. This species has the closest resemblance to My physical imagery, and they call themselves the 'Homo sapiens'. According to the formation of their science, the Homo sapiens are the continuation of another species that did not survive the hostility of their natural environment."

The Esser Yaad continued,

"I must look deep into the depths of their essence to see what physical and metaphysical capability they possess."

Part 7: Then the Esser Yaad looked deep into the depths of their essence, trying to analyse the total capabilities of this species. When this analysation was over, He raised His voice of magic once again and said,

"The visual structure of their physique and the image and size of their brain is appropriate for what I intend to do. I will use the outer layers of their brain and multiply their hidden capability by a zillion times to be correctly relevant for My souls of fire. Now I must return back and proceed with the most important magic of fire, the creation of My souls."

Part 8: So the Esser Yaad returned to the domain of darkness. As He had strategically planned, He kept four images within the centre of His imagination. When these images found their true formation, He projected their visual outlines into the open space directly in front of Himself, upon His mysterious altar of magic.

Part 9: Time, however inconsistent, was passing in the most mystical sense. The Esser Yaad successfully constructed each section of His magical strategy accordingly, and here they were, four mighty structures of metaphysical solidness, right above the altar of fire. But there was one more thing that the Esser Yaad had to do, and that was to inject the seed of vitality and infuse the essence of immortality into each and every one of these created souls of fire.

CHAPTER SEVENTEEN

IN MY BREATH YOU SHALL BREATHE. IN MY FIRE YOU SHALL LIVE

Part 1: So the Esser Yaad constructed the visual images of His souls of fire. Right above the altar of magic were standing firm the four magnificent embodiments of metaphysical solidness, ready to be awakened and become the real inhabitants in the mind of fire.

Part 2: The Esser Yaad, content in the totality of His existence, looked upon the solidness of His created souls of fire. Then He raised His volcanic voice of power and said,

"Excellent! This is precisely what I had in mind. Now I have to infuse the hidden matter with energy. I have to awaken these mighty forces from the state of dreamless sleep, and I must inject the seed of life and the essence of immortality into the very centre of their being.

"Let Me think. This is the most delicate part of My practical mysticism. To complete this final phase, I have to project Myself into the centre of their minds. From there, I should penetrate every existing cell to inject the seed of life and the essence of immortality into the solidness of their very being. When this procedure has been accomplished, I must circulate with the ultimate mode of velocity to create the breathing sequence and then find My way out through the exhalation of their breath. This will complete the first act of creation, the creation of My souls of fire."

Part 3: So the Esser Yaad followed the pattern of His strategy and fulfilled every procedure of this mysticism to the point of ultimate perfection. Then suddenly, the eyes of these newly formed intelligences of fire opened. They were looking deep and mysteriously, directly into the face of the Lord of fire, our celestial hero of the Exordium.

Part 4: When this historical phase of magic was accomplished, the Esser Yaad raised Himself to equal the height of the altar of fire. Then He paused for a very short moment of inconsistent time. He elevated His volcanic voice of power and authorised the first-ever statement of magical awakening in this manner of presentation:

"You are the souls of fire.

"You are the intelligences of Yaad.

"You are personified with the Esser of My name.

"You can see through the altar of My eyes.

"You can hear through the temple of My ears.

"You can speak through the letters of My thought, and you can think through the layers of My mind.

"In My breath you shall breathe. In My fire you shall live."

Part 5: The Esser Yaad, this celestial fire of the Exordium, continued,

"You are the totality, the totality of metaphysical solidness.

"You are the structure, the structure of invincible completeness.

"The direction of My feet is your path to immortality.

"Your hand has the greatness of My seal of power.

"Endless is your emotion.

"Endurance (is) your constitution.

"In My breath you shall breathe. In My fire you shall live."

Part 6: The Esser Yaad, this ultimate personification of constructive fire, continued,

"Your consciousness is exorcitation.

"Your awareness (is) electrification.

"You are indomitable, indomitable in every phase of history.

"You are inimitable, inimitable in every secret of mystery.

"Inexhaustibility is the mode, the mode of your flames.

"Invincibility is the sign, the sign of your names.

"In My breath you shall breathe. In My fire you shall live."

Introduction to Chapters 18-22

In the next few chapters, the Esser Yaad, this ultimate Lord of the Exordium, will begin to introduce each and every single one of these universal souls of fire. The introduction of these original gods is performed in the specific ritual of magic. The Esser Yaad moves clockwise, looking at His souls of fire, naming them accordingly. The first one He names 'Atar-Sheen', the fire of fire. The second one He names 'Serya-Sheen', the fire of mystery. The third one 'Suryim-Sheen', the fire who ceases the extermination. And the forth one He names the 'Yetser-Sheen', the fire who multiplies the infinity.

When the ritual of this introduction was complete, these magnificent images of the hidden history came forth and stood by the altar of fire. One by one, they began to make an oath, establishing the eternal alliance with the Esser Yaad, the ultimate Lord of fire.

The Esser Yaad stands patiently, hearing each and every single one of their praises and promises full-heartedly. At the end of each oath, he gives them their universal mission. He tells them that their first duty is to detect certain spheres of reality so He can construct His future empire, and their second mission is to break the pressure of darkness and locate the eyes of intelligence and the thought-forms of Hee'yaak.

The Esser Yaad reminds these cosmic forces of fire that a continuous connection with Him is essential, and each one of them should choose a certain geometrical image so their telepathical communication with Him would be instantaneous.

Atar-Sheen chooses the geometrical image of the circle. The circle becomes his line of magic. The Serya-Sheen chooses the image of the triangle. The triangle becomes his gate of magic. Suryim-Sheen selects the mysterious image of the square. The square becomes his formation of magic. And the Yetser-Sheen chooses the straight line. The straight line becomes the sign of his geometrical magic.

There are many important concepts in these chapters that the reader should comprehend, but in this summarised commentary, I have selected two significant points to discuss.

First, the Esser Yaad tells the souls of fire that the constant connection with Him is essential. Basically, they should always be in contact as their conquest of darkness depends upon this simple factor. We should learn that we, as individuals, should follow the path of these ancient gods of the hidden world. We should also find the connecting pattern with the Esser Yaad, the Lord of constructive fire.

The second note has magical significance. These four magnificent powers of the universe give us their geometrical images so they can be contacted in the mental, astral and ethereal levels. How to formulate this connection is a complex procedure of magic that I think every member of the human race, every intelligence and every soul of fire should learn.

I know that through the advancement of the human mentality a new age of spiritual evolution will begin. Possibly this is one of the reasons why the Exordium has been sent into the world.

Hopefully, people will heed the call of this book. They will conquer every sphere of thought. They will unlock every key of consciousness and they will complete every division of magic so they can stand above the fishes of the sea, the birds of the sky and the beasts of the field. Let us hope for emergence of that day.

So be it.

CHAPTER EIGHTEEN

Now Is The Time That You Step Into The Memory Of The Universe

Part 1: So the Esser Yaad successfully accomplished the first act of creation. When this practical phase of mystery was complete and the first statement of magical awakening was presented accordingly, these four intelligences of universal solidness began to move in a circular motion. They were creating a cycle of multicoloured light around the totality of the Esser Yaad, the Lord of the constructive fire.

Part 2: After the completion of this mysterious procedure, they stood firm above the ground of the Underworld. They were waiting patiently to hear the voice of the Esser Yaad who was preparing to dictate yet another statement of historical mysticism. The Esser Yaad broke the silence in the absolute mode of thoughtfulness and began the next series of His magical conversation in this manner of discourse:

"Now is the time that you step into the memory of the universe. This is the aeon that you will become one with the entirety of existence, and this is the moment that you shall receive the sign of eliteness and the title of your universal identity."

Part 3: Then this constructive Lord of Exordium looked towards the first intelligence of fire and said,

"Your name and infinite seal of power is 'Atar-Sheen', the fire of fire."

346

As He moved clockwise, he stopped, facing the second intelligence of fire, and said,

"Your mystical name of invincibility is 'Serya-Sheen', the fire of mystery."

The Esser Yaad continued His mysterious motion until He faced the third intelligence of celestial solidness. Then He paused attentively and said,

"Your mysterious name and the unconquerable title of recognition is 'Suryim-Sheen', the fire that ceases the extermination."

The Esser Yaad still eloquently followed His magical pattern of mystery until He reached the fourth and final intelligence of fire and said,

"Your magical name and indestructible equation of identity is 'Yetser-Sheen', the fire that multiplies the infinity."

Part 4: The Esser Yaad still continued,

"Now this is the most significant moment of awakening. Let us glorify the future path of this constructive certainty. Let us celebrate the existing cycle of this rising reality and let us imprint the letters of wonder upon the hidden particles of so-called history. Let us proceed."

CHAPTER NINETEEN

THE ATAR-SHEEN, THE FIRE OF FIRE

Part 1: So the Esser Yaad completed the first ritual of His magic. When this procedure was complete, the atmosphere within this domain of mystery changed in the most constructive sense. There was a pause of silence, but this silence was the silence of the rising flames of glory.

Part 2: Suddenly, the Atar-Sheen, the fire of fire, came forth. With the absolute mode of eloquence, he raised his voice of integrity and said,

"Esser Yaad, You are the master of this created domain of existence. I live within the fire of Your breath and I exist through the solidness of Your mind. I want to be within the totality of Your oneness. I want to witness what Your magic can create. I want to see which words of light You utter. I want to recognise the mystery that You unfold, and I want to touch the visible thoughts that Your imagination formulates. I am ready to fulfil my mission. I know the path is infinite and the route is coarse; but I promise to the flames of my fire, and I make an oath to Your secret name of power, that my union with Your authority is unbreakable. I am in perfect alliance with the majesty of Your soul. To me, You are the founder of creation and the breath behind the evolution of any constructive consciousness."

Part 3: Then the Esser Yaad, this Lord of constructive fire, raised His voice of glory and said,

"Blessing be upon your soul. Your first mission is to go forth and detect a suitable domain of reality so we can construct the universal empire of evolution, and your second mission is to break the intensity of darkness and locate the position of the Hee'yaak, the thought-forms of animation; and the Seypher, the eyes of intelligence. When your missions are accomplished, you can return. Meanwhile, whatever significant occurrences you confront or you witness on your voyage to infinity, project them into My mind through the picturographic satellite mechanism[1] that is installed within the depths of your intelligence. Remember, the continuous connection with Me is essential. To be able to do this, you should select a certain geometrical formula so your telepathical communication with the flames of My fire would be instantaneous."

Part 4: Then after a very short moment of inconsistent time, the Atar-Sheen, this fire of fire, nodded his head attentively and said,

"My geometrical image of mystery is the circle. I will come into Your mind through the circle of fire. I will come into Your mind through the circle of fire."

---

[1] Picturographic satellite mechanism: some form of mental telepathy

CHAPTER TWENTY

THE SERYA-SHEEN, THE FIRE OF MYSTERY

Part 1: In this chapter, we enter the moment when the second structure of intelligence came forth into this cycle of magic. When the atmosphere became ready for the next dialogue, the Serya-Sheen, the fire of mystery, selected his words with the absolute mode of eloquence and said,

"Esser Yaad, You are the architect of my created soul. The reality of this existence depends upon the solidness of Your imagination. Within Your breath I shall breathe. Within Your fire I shall live. I want to be within the temple of Your mind. I want to rise within the emotion of Your heart, and I want to see the effect of Your mystic hand that constructs the passages of possibilities. Esser Yaad, I promise to the flames of my fire and I make an oath to Your hidden name of power that my alliance with Your essence of divinity is absolute. To me, You are the all-knowing force of immortality and the genesis of awakening."

Part 2: When the statement of Serya-Sheen was completed in the most honourable sense, the Esser Yaad raised His magical voice of glory and said,

"Blessing be upon your soul. You also have two missions to accomplish: first is to go above and see if you can detect any form of solid ground on which we can construct the universal empire of evolution; and your second mission is to go forth into

351

the illusion of darkness and locate the position of the Hee'yaak, the thought-forms of animation; and the Seypher, the eyes of intelligence. Serya-Sheen, in this voyage of mystery, whatever significant occurrences you confront or witness, project them into My mind through the picturographic satellite instrument that is hidden within the totality of your consciousness. Remember, connection with Me is the most essential pattern to victory. To be able to maintain this connection, you should select your own geometrical formula so your telepathical communication with the flames of My fire would be immediate."

Part 3: Then the Serya-Sheen closed his eyes for a very short moment of inconsistent time. He concentrated and went through the first procedure of thoughtfulness. When this procedure was over, he opened his eyes of mystery and said,

"My geometrical image of connection is the triangle. I come into Your mind through the central point and the mystical gate of the triangle. I come into Your mind through the mystical gate of the triangle."

CHAPTER TWENTY ONE

THE SURYIM-SHEEN, THE FIRE WHO CEASES THE EXTERMINATION

Part 1: When the second structure of intelligence had selected his geometrical image of mystery, again the sensation of silence encompassed this domain of magic. As every particle of this hidden zone was at ease, Suryim-Sheen, the fire who ceases the extermination, came forth to open a new dialogue of alliance. He began his discourse in this manner of presentation:

"Esser Yaad, You are the totality, the totality of the emerging universe. The realistic solidness of my touchable soul depends upon the existence of Your imagination. I shall breathe through the breath of Your name, and I shall live within the greatness of Your essence. I want to be the image of perfection within the entirety of Your thought. I want to be the dream of reality within the centre of Your consciousness. And I want to see the effect of Your ark that passes through the intensity of darkness. Esser Yaad, I promise to the flames of my fire, and I make an oath to Your sacred title of mystery that my alliance with Your soul of divinity is unbreakable. To me, You are the eternal oneness of creation and the architect behind the equation of immortality."

Part 2: When the Suryim-Sheen's dialogue of universal alliance was complete, the Esser Yaad raised His magical voice of authority and said,

"Blessing be upon your soul. You, Suryim-Sheen, the flame of power and the shield of rising fire, also have two sophisticated missions to accomplish. First, to penetrate into the right-hand side of this darkness to see if you can detect any region with the solid foundation so we can construct the future empire; and your second mission is to search within the totality of the Underworld to locate the positions of the Hee'yaak, the thought-forms of animation; and the locations of the Seypher, the eyes of intelligence. Suryim-Sheen, whatever significant occurrences that emerge in your way, or that you witness through your voyage to infinity, project them into My mind through the picturographic satellite mechanism that is at the very centre of your consciousness. Remember, constant connection with Me is the most essential instrument of victory. To be able to maintain this mode of connection, chose one geometrical formula so that your telepathical communication with the flames of My thought would be without any form of delay."

Part 3: Then the Suryim-Sheen, this fire that ceases the extermination, concentrated for a very short amount of inconsistent time. When this momentary concentration was over, he raised his voice of eloquence in the absolute mode of certainty and said,

"My geometrical image of connection is the shape of the square. I will come into Your mind through the heart of this image and the centre of this four-sided shape of mystery. I will come to You through the centre of the square."

CHAPTER TWENTY TWO

THE YETSER-SHEEN, THE FIRE THAT MULTIPLIES THE INFINITY

Part 1: When the mysterious conversation between the Esser Yaad and Suryim-Sheen was complete, the Yetser-Sheen, the fire that multiplies the infinity, came forth. He stood on the left-hand side of the altar of magic. He raised his voice of eloquence in the absolute mode of thoughtfulness and said,

"Esser Yaad, You are the foundation of my mystic soul. You are the multiplicity of any form of constructive consciousness, and You are the sign of awakening who created the path for metaphysical perfection. In Your breath I shall always breathe, and in Your fire I shall eternally live. I want to be within the centre, the centre of Your awareness. I want to become the structure of thought within the solidness of Your memory, and I want to see Your mathematical intelligence that creates the scientific accuracy. Esser Yaad, I know the darkness is diffusing and the voyage is rough, but my mind is set. Your mission is my mission. I promise to the flames of my fire, and I make an oath to Your magnificent name of magic that my alliance with Your essence of immortality is ultimate. To me, You are the indefinable power of persistency. You are the glory of eminence and the centre of visibility."

Part 2: Then the Esser Yaad, this constructive Lord of fire and this ultimate hero of the Exordium, raised His magical voice of glory and said,

"Blessing be upon your soul. You are the ultimate equation of identity. You, Yetser-Sheen, who multiplies the infinity, also have two universal missions to accomplish. First, to surge into the left-hand side of the Underworld to see if you can detect any domain of stability so we can create the future empire of light; and your second mission is to detect the location of the Hee'yaak, the thought-forms of animation; and the Seypher, the eyes of intelligence. Yetser-Sheen, you are the intelligence of fire. Any significant occurrences that come in your way, or any incident that you may encounter on your voyage to infinity, project them into My mind through the picturographic satellite mechanism that is at the very centre of your hidden brain. Remember, and have in mind, that the constant connection is the first law to succeed. Now select one geometrical formula so the telepathical communication with the flames of My fire would be immediate and without a delay."

Part 3: The time passed in the most mystical sense. Yetser-Sheen concentrated thoughtfully and then raised his voice of mystery in the ultimate mode of precision and presented his statement in this manner of discourse:

"My geometrical image of distinction is the straight line. I come into Your mind through the diameter of this shape and the verticality of this image of completeness. I come into Your mind through the verticality of the straight line."

Part 4: When Yetser-Sheen presented his practical image of connection, the Esser Yaad looked upon His souls of fire in the absolute mode of thoughtfulness. Then He raised His voice of power and said,

"From this moment of inconsistent time, we are all part of one mission, one destiny. We are all the solid structure of the first network of construction. We should all go forth to exercise the solidness of our souls. We should surge into the darkness to reach the other end of eternity. So let us proceed."

TO BE CONTINUED...

THE EXORDIUM

THE PROPHECY FULFILLED

Part 1: In the next volume, the emergence of the gods continues and the war for supremacy begins. Typhoon launches his campaign to control the darkness and sit upon the throne of power. Many other intelligences of darkness are born: more complete, more intelligent and more destructive than before. Amongst them, Sereph-Taaz, the slithery character of deceit, will create the first negative alliance of the Underworld; Nifu, the wind of destruction, will come to destroy everything in his path; and the Gereh will manifest as the fearsome characteristic of metaphysical death.

We will meet a force of bitterness and vengeance named Sotai who claims that the gods had cheated him and stolen his birthright. And finally the most terrible mind of negativity, the Epep, the titanic snake of the Underworld, will slither from the depths of the Abyss to impose His will over the inhabitants of this forgotten universe.

As these destructive and sinister characters emerge, the Underworld becomes the chaos where only the strongest and most clever can survive.

Within this darkness, many constructive forces of divinity enter to assist the strategy of creation: Zaman, the god of time who rules over the cycles of age; Sai Isa, the Lord of compassion; Numiyas, the calculating force who dominates the sphere of precision; and Om-Heh, the universal sound of peace.

As for the souls of fire, they begin to carry out their missions within the darkness. But as there is no escaping the presence of the negative intelligences, they must clash against the armies of destruction. In this climate of the unknown, the Esser Yaad analyses the difficulties of the Underworld, strategises anew and then the second cycle of the gods of the ancient aeon are born.

Part 2: We will hear more from the writer, Mehdi Zand, as he speaks with the Esser Yaad, and many questions will be answered about his mysterious connection to this ultimate force of the divine.

In the second volume, a new gate of philosophy is opened. Many series of conversations take place between the writer, Mehdi Zand, and the Lord of the Exordium, the Esser Yaad. In their enlightening discussions, the controversy reaches a different level as Mehdi Zand expresses his views on the current state of the world.

So what is his view? What does he think of world politics? Who does he say he is? What is his view of religion? Is the Lord of the Exordium the same god as people worship today? Well, read the second volume and go into a new journey, the journey into the depths of mystery and reality.

If you found the Emergence of the Gods controversial, then prepare yourself for the Exordium, Volume 2: The Prophecy Fulfilled. This was just the beginning – the best is yet to come. The gods, once more, are waiting.